The Book of

Love, Laughter & Romance

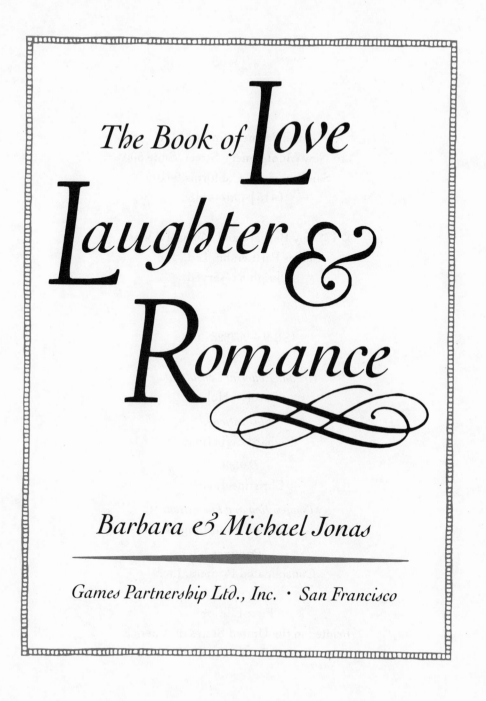

The Book of Love Laughter & Romance

Barbara & Michael Jonas

Games Partnership Ltd., Inc. · San Francisco

Games Partnership Ltd., Inc.
116 New Montgomery Street, Suite 500
San Francisco, California 94105
[415] 495-4411

ISBN 0-9638281-0-X

Art and Editorial Consultant:
Carolyn Holm

Illustrations:
Richard Sigberman

Design:
Christine Taylor

Composition and Production:
Wilsted & Taylor Publishing Services

Printing:
Consolidated Printers, Inc.

First Edition
Printed in the United States of America
10 9 8 7 6 5 4 3 2 1

To our parents,
Gertrude Bricklin and Albert Bricklin,
Janet Jonas and Norman Jonas,
whose values, attitudes, and love
help shape our lives and make them richer

Acknowledgments

Writing this book was exciting, challenging, stimulating, and, at times, simply exhausting. But this book would not have come into existence without the help, guidance, and encouragement of a number of people, not least of whom were the couples who enthusiastically gave us so much wonderful information.

Our deepest gratitude goes to Carolyn Holm, our "impresario" and editor, who brought order to chaos and in so many ways helped shape this book, and whose tireless and unflagging effort and enthusiasm kept the process going; to Richard Sigberman, whose lovely illustrations have captured visually what we've tried to say in words; to Christine Taylor of Wilsted & Taylor Publishing Services, who, with patience and tact, helped give this book its form and color; and to Dennis Briskin, whose "wordsmithing" and sense of humor were invaluable.

We'd also like to thank Angela Jackson, Christie Hurta, and Carmen Lim at Games Partnership, whose recommendations and support (to say nothing of their patience) were so helpful to us.

And, we'd like to extend a very special thanks to the thousands of couples who shared their stories, ideas, and suggestions with us, and for whom the fire of romance continues to burn brightly. Without them there would be no book.

Contents

INTRODUCTION

Why We Wrote

The Book of Love, Laughter & Romance

He couldn't wait to go, and I couldn't wait for him to leave.

A disagreement, a misunderstanding, and we had found ourselves in the middle of an argument. The timing couldn't have been worse. Michael had to leave on a five-day business trip before we could resolve things, and wouldn't be back until early New Year's Eve.

Michael and I had been married sixteen years, and had spent virtually every New Year's Eve privately and quietly at home together, staying awake just long enough to toast each other at midnight. However, it looked as though this new year might have a bumpy start.

What we needed, when he returned home, was a way for us to refocus on what we like and love about each other and put the argument behind us.

While he was away, I hit on an idea that would accomplish just that. I designed a game. Little did I know that it would also change our lives.

Over the next few days, I wrote out game cards with questions that would invite us to talk about what attracts us to each other, and suggestions that would encourage us to gently touch. Then I made a small game board that would literally bring us closer together.

On the afternoon Michael was due back, I went out for groceries, and, along with food for a special dinner, came back with an armload of chrysanthemums, a bottle of champagne, candles, fresh strawberries (an out-of-season extravagance that seemed perfect for the occasion), and a large bag of M&M's,™ his favorite candy.

I put wood and kindling in the fireplace, carefully arranged the flowers in vases, placed candles generously around the room, and chilled the champagne. The room was transformed.

I taped a note on the front door suggesting that he freshen up from his trip and meet me in the living room. Meanwhile, I changed into something silky that makes me feel especially attractive. Then I lit the kindling and the candles, dimmed the lights, and put on soft jazz. When I was done, the setting seemed magical to me . . . I hoped that he would see it the same way.

On the one hand I was looking forward to coming home from the trip. On the other hand, I was also dreading it. I didn't want to face the unresolved tension if it were still there. I was worried that our usually intimate New Year's Eve celebration would be spoiled, until I read the note on the door (". . . meet me in the living room"). What was she planning? Intrigued, I followed her instructions.

Barbara looked absolutely stunning sitting in the living room bathed in the glow of soft, flickering can-

dlelight. The air was filled with the sweet aroma of flowers and the sound of some of my favorite saxophone music. Food and champagne were attractively arranged. It was clear that Barbara had gone to considerable effort to make this happen, and I thought how wonderful it is to be loved and appreciated this much. She did this all for me — for us!

And Barbara's game . . .

She invited me to sit down on the rug with her in front of the fireplace. Her directions were simple — we each were to take a Wish Card (actually an index card) and write down a secret wish. "Something that can be fulfilled before the night is out," she suggested. "I'll do the same, and the winner will be granted his or her wish."

We took turns drawing the game cards she'd prepared. The first card read:

> *It might be pizza on a rainy night or a sunset on a beach; describe a magic moment you've shared with your partner.*

And so the game began.
Other cards followed —

> *H. G. Wells' Time Machine is in your driveway. Where in history would you like to rendezvous with your partner?*

> *Using the tip of a finger and your most flowery style — trace your name somewhere on your partner's body.*

> *The future includes hopes and dreams — what three things do you hope your partner will experience this year?*

> *The 'How Much Feeling Can You Put into a Kiss Contest' has just begun. You are a contestant. Give your partner the winning kiss.*

We played, laughed, talked, and touched. The argument evaporated. And the experience we shared —intimate, intense, and moving—brought us closer together than ever.

When friends and relatives asked us about our New Year's Eve, we told them about the game. Everyone was intrigued. We loaned out the homemade game to friends who wanted to try it.

At 7:30 one morning, the phone rang. It was our friends who had borrowed the game the day before, and they were going on and on about what a wonderful experience they'd had.

We loaned the game to more and more friends and relatives. Everyone who played it, loved it. That's when we began to see that we were on to something. And we realized that if they found it so wonderful, so would other couples. From this, we created the game *An Enchanting Evening*.

Now, years later, the game has been played by more than 500,000 couples of all ages, married or dating, with and without children. Some have discovered the game while vacationing in a hotel that offers it to guests as part of a romantic weekend package. Some have been given the game as a wedding or anniversary gift. Others have heard about it from friends, relatives, clergy, and marriage and family counselors. *An Enchanting Evening* has become THE romance game now sold throughout the world.

But the story doesn't end here. People not only played the game but also wanted to share their feelings about it. Thousands of notes, letters, postcards, and phone calls came in from people telling us how much they enjoyed *An Enchanting Evening*. Many of the people who contacted us went beyond the game to describe the many other ways they add spark and zest to their relationship.

This outpouring of shared romantic experiences astonished us and everyone we told about it. As stories and testimonials kept coming in, we became a sort of unofficial clearinghouse for romantic suggestions! To share the riches, we decided to put them all together in a book so that others could benefit from these ideas.

To expand and enhance the material we'd collected, we went back to the couples who had written to us and asked them to complete an in-depth questionnaire about how they celebrate romance. We interviewed many of them by telephone, and we held informal gatherings to talk about romance. We were inundated with wit and wisdom, colorful stories, humorous anecdotes, thoughtful philosophizing, and practical, down-to-earth ideas for romantic things to do together.

The result is an overflowing cornucopia of romantic suggestions for celebrating relationships. What these suggestions all have in common is that they are true, coming from real people who have used these ideas to add fun and excitement, poetry and music to their lives together.

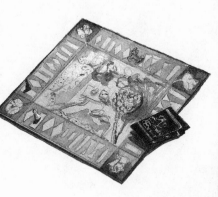

The ideas are as varied as their contributors — men and women of all ages, in all types of relationships, in different stages of their lives: dating, engaged, recently married, married for years, with or without children, two-career couples, couples in retirement . . . we heard from them all.

Like couples everywhere, they sometimes feel pressured by work, children, money, and all the other demands of daily life. Yet they all find ways to enrich their relationships by keeping romance alive.

We know you'll find many ways to use this book. Some people will keep it by their bedside as a "pillow book." Some will take turns reading parts aloud to their partner. Some will turn down a page, or leave a bookmark, at a special place for their partner to read.

Our offering is a delicious buffet of ideas, suggestions, and activities. Some will appeal to you immediately. Others may prompt only a nibble (at least for now). Still others may provide inspiration for you to "cook up" your own romantic treats. Go back to the buffet as often as you wish — and enjoy!

Note

In collecting the materials for this book, we received letters and cards from thousands of couples. We also spoke individually with people, conducted discussion groups, and asked participants to fill out written questionnaires.

In doing so, we promised that we would protect their confidentiality by altering the details of the information we were given.

Because the suggestions and advice we received came in all shapes and sizes — from the short note to the very detailed letter — we've taken the liberty of editing, condensing, combining, and rewriting this information to make it accessible to our readers.

The Book of

Love, Laughter & Romance

What Is This Thing Called Romance?

I think it was the longest trade show I'd ever attended — a true test of endurance. Then my flight back was delayed. I wasn't sure which was worse, my gnawing hunger, my frazzled nerves, or my aching feet and legs.

Finally home, I dropped my luggage in the entry hall and closed the front door behind me. I was greeted with a big, warm bear hug. He sat me down, took off my shoes, and then made me a cup of tea to revive me while he finished making dinner. No more coffee shop and airplane food — a simple pasta dish and salad never tasted so good.

"Love in your heart wasn't put there to stay, Love isn't love 'til you give it away."
Oscar Hammerstein II

That's romance!

My husband had major surgery and was going to
be flat on his back. I thought of what I could bring
to the hospital for him to have at his bedside. I
selected some special things that he would enjoy:
an aromatic sprig of lavender from our garden,
a framed picture of our family (including him as
he'd look when he felt better again), a portable
recorder with a few of his favorite tapes, and a
small book of poetry we both enjoy.

During his stay in the hospital, I'd close the
door, hold his hand, and quietly read poetry.

That's romance!

I was stuck in another traffic tie-up on the bridge.
I told myself not to get aggravated and opened the
glove compartment to take out a cassette . . .
music to calm this savage beast. Inside was a tape
with a bow on it, but no label. Curious, I slipped
the tape into the player.

I heard my wife's voice. She had taped a
selection of my favorite Western songs, introducing them like a D.J., but with personal comments,
and a dedication "to the one I love." Suddenly,
the traffic jam seemed much less stressful.

*"Love is an
irresistible desire
to be irresistibly
desired."*
Robert Frost

That's romance!

THE REWARDS
OF ROMANCE

*Adds spice . . . sparkle
. . . zest to our lives*

•

Hugs, kisses, caressing

•

*Feeling attractive
to my partner*

•

*Our relationship
flourishes*

•

Holds us together

•

Keeps us close

•

*Provides intimacy
and caring*

•

*Deepens our
appreciation and love
for one another*

•

Keeps things fresh

•

*Makes our daily
routines more
than bearable*

Songs have been written about it, florists thrive on it, and candy manufacturers couldn't survive without it. But romance is far more than love lyrics, long-stemmed roses, and chocolate bonbons.

Romance means different things to different people, and it's expressed in infinite ways. When we spoke with couples, they described romance to us using many words: "love," "consideration," "fun," "mischief," sometimes "surprise." Some talked of shared time, shared activities. Others mentioned their underlying passion for their partner.

But it's the prospect of intimacy that seems to be the foundation of romance, whether acted upon or not. No one has trouble distinguishing the considerate gesture that you make to a friend, a parent, or a child from the one that you call "romantic." It's that underlying intimacy that makes a look or an act romantic, as subtle or as heady as a lingering fragrance.

But that's just a part of it.

What we kept hearing from couples is that romance is also a way of making the "everyday" special. Of making the relationship special. Of making each other feel special. Of making an occasion special.

One Order of Valentines

Last February we had to travel out of state on business. On our way back, we were forced to lay over in Denver during a snowstorm. We were sitting in the airport coffee shop waiting for our breakfast order, too tired to even talk. I didn't notice that my husband had gotten up to speak with the waitress. When she put a plate of heart-shaped pancakes in front of me, my husband broke into a big smile and squeezed my hand. "Happy Valentine's!" I had completely forgotten that it was the 14th!

Romance is not so much *what* these people do, as what they bring to it: their attitude. They all find romantic ways to make their partner feel appreciated. For one person, appreciation is a bunch of daisies on a breakfast tray; for another it's a slow, tender massage; for a third it's surprising his wife by washing her car. Each notion of a romantic gesture is quite different; but the attitude expressed is what they all have in common.

Anyone can be romantic; the ways to be romantic are endless! You're not limited to roses and candy. It's almost any act that says "I love you," "I care about you," "I appreciate you."

THE REWARDS OF ROMANCE

*Brings fun and joy
to our relationship*

•

Helps love grow

•

*Warms our hearts and
keeps our souls alive*

•

*Lets us hear the little
things we love to hear*

•

Makes us each feel sexy

•

*Makes me feel special
. . . valued*

•

*Provides an atmosphere
of mutual support*

•

*Keeps our marriage
from being "all work"*

•

*Reminds us how lucky
we are to be sharing life
and love together*

*"Love is a
friendship
set to music."*

E. Joseph Cossman

A Charming Thought

My husband had an important presentation to make. He practiced at home all weekend, going through his slides and flip charts. On Monday morning he was visibly nervous. For good luck, he wore the tie the kids and I gave him for Father's Day. We sent him off to work with a chorus of "Knock their socks off!" He was planning to drive to work for the morning, and then he'd drive to the client's office for the presentation after lunch. Later that morning, I went by his office parking lot and left a rabbit's foot key chain under his windshield wiper. He had won it at a carnival when he was a kid and it had been sitting around in this and that drawer over the years. I thought that might give him a little lift.

If romance is so wonderful and welcomed, why aren't we all romantic all the time? Many people have very thoughtful answers to this question. People described the stresses and strains of full schedules. They talked about the impact of children on a relationship. They spoke of how easy it is, over time, to slide into the habit of not making the effort.

Yet we also heard over and over how wonderful it is when they do make that effort, no matter how seemingly small the gesture.

What do they receive in return for making the effort? Every couple speaks of the power of romance to strengthen their relationship. One refers to it as the glue that binds them together, another as the spark that sets a roaring bonfire. Several describe romance as the seasoning that adds spice to their relationship. For others it's what gives intimacy meaning. For each couple, the richness that romance brings is a powerful incentive to keep it a part of their lives.

These are real people. They work, take care of their families, face disappointments, and juggle the day-to-day problems and challenges of life. And even with all of this, they continue to keep their relationships vital and strong, satisfying and exciting, interesting and challenging, and, above all, filled with love, by never losing sight of the important role that romance plays in their lives.

"The Eskimos have 52 names for snow because it was important to them; there ought to be as many for love."
Margaret Atwood

Grace Notes

My wife plays the violin and I play piano. When one of us is on tour, we like to leave little notes tucked into each other's music or instrument cases. Being musicians, we tend to use musical terms and metaphors, so somewhere along the line we started referring to these as grace notes.

A grace note is a small, extra note that embellishes a musical piece. A grace note can also be a form of intimate communication that enriches a relationship; it's a way of saying to each other, "You're on my mind."

"All of the beautiful sentiments in the world weigh less than a single lovely action."
James Russell Lowell

A Treasure

We've been married for fifty-seven years, and one
of our great pleasures has been the writing of little
notes to each other. On lovely cards, stationery,
fine letter paper . . . but also on the backs of old
tickets, laundry slips, used envelopes. We write
simple things just to say "I'm thinking of you."
Some are corny, especially when we try to
be humorous. Some are more thoughtful —
expressions of deeply held feelings. But we've
never thrown away a single note — not in all
these years.

And our children know that. For our fiftieth
anniversary they gave us a large, beautifully
decorated leather box to hold our treasure.

Couples talked about how they surprise each other with messages, left at unexpected times or places around the house. They send notes to each other in the mail, leave notes on the pillow, on the workbench, in the medicine cabinet . . . notes that say thank you for something, for anything, or for nothing in particular. Notes that are funny, serious, tender, even silly. And, of course, everyone appreciates a compliment!

You can make a card. It doesn't have to be fancy to convey your feelings; that you cared enough to make it is a message in itself. A little sketch, a poem, a limerick, a calligraphic flourish . . . on special paper or with an unusually colored ink, perhaps scented with your favorite fragrance or aftershave to make it even more personal.

You can borrow from others. Almost anyone can make a charming card by cutting and pasting pictures, words, or headlines out of magazines. Or you can put your effort into finding just the right store-bought card.

"I always work very hard at finding a sentiment that I truly feel in the cards I give. I'm not as creative as my husband — he likes to make cards — but I feel that I'm creative in finding just the right one."

"The manner of giving is worth more than the gift."
Pierre Corneille

THE WRITTEN WORD

*Love notes . . . formal,
informal . . .
in a special place . . .
or hidden,
waiting to be found*

•

*Greeting cards . . .
serious, whimsical,
risqué . . .
carefully selected,
or made yourself*

•

*Letters . . . because
one of you is away,
or just because*

•

*Poems . . . something
you read and love
or something from
your heart and pen*

Notes Everywhere

Whenever I go out of town, I like to leave notes near the coffeepot, on top of the TV, near his shaving cream, even in the freezer. It's my way of reminding him how much I love him and that he's in my thoughts.

Sometimes I slip notes into his shirt or jacket pocket in the morning for him to find during the day. "Hello; remember me? I love you."

———◆◆◆———

From time to time I put notes in her briefcase. Once, when she was conducting an important meeting, she reached in and pulled out some papers with my note attached. She says she blushed when she saw it, but managed to keep going without skipping a beat. She doesn't think anyone noticed!

———◆◆◆———

Every morning I pack my husband's lunch. Once in a while, I write a really "spicy" note on his napkin.

———◆◆◆———

We work in offices across town from each other. But occasionally I have a chance to go by the lot where he parks his car and leave a note on his windshield. Just a few words to say that I'm thinking of him.

———◆◆◆———

I like to leave a trail of notes. She finds the first one in some obvious place — like next to her coffee cup. That leads to another note, and the next, and so on until finally the last one invites her out to dinner.

I use those little Post-Its™ for notes I can leave everywhere around the house. When he cleaned the car recently, I put one on the dashboard saying, "Thank you; I love you."

We like to order out from a nearby Chinese restaurant. I asked them where they get their fortune cookies and then called the factory to place a special order: a dozen cookies, each with a "private" message inside. The next time we ordered Chinese food, I switched the cookies, replacing those from the restaurant with the ones I special-ordered. I told her that someone at the factory must be flirting with her, but I don't think she believed me.

THE WRITTEN WORD

Post-Its™ . . . stuck here, stuck there

•

Lipstick . . . on a mirror

•

Calligraphy . . . for an artful flourish

•

An ad in the newspaper . . . for a dramatic flourish

•

Chalkboard . . . a daily message or a once-in-a-while surprise

•

Refrigerator magnets . . . a daily message or a now-and-then surprise

During the workday, grace notes not only make your hours brighter, but they also bring the two of you closer at the day's end. Notes tucked into a briefcase or lunch box . . . a call in the afternoon to keep in touch.

Modern technology has given romantic couples a whole new array of methods: answering machines to leave messages at work (as long as the answering system is private), or as a greeting when coming home to an empty house; voice mail; pagers with private signals; even faxes, if appropriate.

High-Tech Grace Notes

When I know my boyfriend's going to have a hectic day at work—meetings, deadlines—I call the night before and leave a voice mail "love note."

We use special codes on our beepers. No one else knows what they mean, but we know they mean "I'm thinking of you."

When we're both at work, sometimes she calls home and leaves me a message on our answering machine. Once she sang "our song." Often she says a few words about how much she loves me.

My husband makes cards and banners for me on his computer. I came home one evening to find a banner across the dining room—"Happy 2,694th Day Together!" He sometimes says he wishes he were more artistic, but I think he should get a prize for pure thoughtfulness.

WHEN ONE OF YOU MUST TRAVEL

Calls . . . frequent and brief, or lingering conversations

•

Messages . . . there when he or she checks in

•

Flowers . . . ever eloquent . . . anywhere, everywhere

•

Letters . . . to anticipate, to be saved, and to be read over and over and over . . .

•

Audio tape . . . the familiar sound of your voice, the sentimental sound of your special music

•

Welcome Home sign . . . a banner . . . poster . . . flag

BEING TOGETHER APART

When you're separated for longer intervals, such as by business travel or family events, reaching out to each other in some way bridges the distance and time you're apart, making each other feel special and appreciated. The telephone is everywhere, but an old-fashioned letter or flowers can also speak for you. Or you can make an audio tape . . . chatting, reading, or playing selections of your special music. And don't forget that a big "Welcome Home" sign can make your returning partner glow.

Picture Perfect

When my wife and kids went to Tennessee to visit her dad, I knew I was going to miss them a lot. But I simply couldn't get away from my work to go with them. Before she left, she gave me a picture of herself and another one of the three girls. On hers she wrote, "I'll be thinking of you every day." On the girls' she wrote, "Daddy, we'll miss you." I kept them in my desk drawer at work, and several times a day I'd find myself glancing at them.

Hotel Room Blues

I don't travel very often on business, but about once a year I have to go to a conference out of town. After a while, the food all starts tasting the same. I sometimes feel that I just can't face one more night out with everyone talking shop.

And I really miss my wife. The last time I went, I was feeling very sorry for myself, alone in my hotel room. So I sat there and wrote her a letter. About how I missed her. About how pretty she is. About how I wished I were there to see her, like when she's reading — she gets so involved — and doesn't know I'm looking at her.

When he came home and gave me this letter he'd written, I was floored. I knew he loved me, but he'd never said anything like this, not in words, not in black and white. His letter was the most beautiful present he's ever given me.

OTHER GRACE NOTES

*Holding hands,
linking arms*

•

*Mealtime magic . . .
make your partner's
favorite "comfort" food
. . . "arousal" food . . .
"indulgence" food*

•

*Songs . . .
play a favorite,
or make one up*

•

*Flirting . . .
just because*

•

*Flowers . . . delivered
or hand picked . . .
placed in the bedroom,
the bathroom,
a lunch box, under a
windshield wiper*

•

Gifts . . . just because

While many couples often write grace notes — notes to each other, a message on a mirror, a journal written together — grace notes don't have to be written. They can be the playing of "your" song or an unexpected kiss on the nape of the neck, flowers for no particular reason, or a surprise gift.

"I like to say 'I love you' by giving her a special gift out of the blue, when there is no occasion."

A Closet Surprise

Once a week we play racquetball together after work. Recently, when we got home I asked him to hang up my coat so I could get started with dinner. He refused! I was so ticked off that I stomped dramatically to the closet and hung it up myself. "Did you hang up your coat?" he asked.

"Yes," I answered curtly.

"Well, you'd better check it again," he said.

Now I was completely exasperated. I flung the closet open again with such force that a package fell at my feet. It was a beautifully wrapped gift with my name on it. He stood there grinning as I opened it and found a handsome sweater, just my color and style. There was no special occasion. He just saw it and knew that I'd like it.

Couples were unanimous in saying flowers are always perfect grace notes.

"I like to give her flowers, not just for special occasions, but now and then as a surprise."

Part of the charm, and much of the message, comes from the surprise of getting flowers on an "ordinary" day (which is now, of course, no longer ordinary).

Flower Time

I'd had a very busy week and Saturday morning was time to sleep in, doze, be lazy. I was only slightly awake when I thought I smelled fresh flowers. I reached out to turn the clock toward me — there, on the table, next to the clock, was a lovely bowl with a gardenia floating in it. I hadn't put it there! Surprised, I propped myself up on my elbow as my husband came in, leaned over, and gave me a kiss.

Bouquet for My Beau

A voice on the office intercom requested that I come to the reception area. I went, thinking an overnight letter had come in for me. At the front desk was a tremendous bouquet of flowers — a riot of color. I assumed one of the women in the office was being courted.

I can still recall how hot my face became when the receptionist said the flowers were for me. The whole work area applauded as I took them back to my office.

I know that it's men who usually send flowers to women, and maybe that's why I felt a bit embarrassed. But to tell you the truth, I loved it!

When you're out together in public there are all sorts of ways to communicate with each other, whether anyone else knows or not. A surreptitious wink, the squeeze of a hand, or a gaze held just long enough speaks privately to both of you while everyone else remains oblivious.

"The melody is in the eyes."
Nicolas Ray

A Sign of the Times

When I was pregnant with our first child, I started going into labor just as my parents dropped by unexpectedly. The contractions were still very mild and slow, so we didn't announce it. We didn't want everyone getting hysterical. Instead, we created a signal between us to time the contractions discreetly.

The signal worked so well that we started to use it to communicate something far more romantic. Now we can say "I love you" privately to each other, across a room, over a table, in the middle of a crowd, just by laying an index finger on one cheek.

Even though they may not be "small," there's also the pleasure of a very public "private" message . . . a radio request, a song request at a restaurant, an ad in the newspaper. Or even more extravagant, for a "big" message, a banner across a highway, a skywriter, or even a blimp. And while your partner may say he or she is embarrassed . . .

The Toast

We were out to dinner with three other couples when, after the wine was served, my husband proposed a toast. "To the love of my life, who also happens to be the Salesperson of the Year." While it was true that I had just won an award at work, I hadn't told any of our friends yet.

His announcement embarrassed me a little, but the recognition of my accomplishment really felt wonderful.

He loves me and is proud of me. I'll take that kind of embarrassment any day.

Most of these grace notes need just a minimum of effort. But as one man, who's been married for over ten years, told us, "Communication bears such sweet fruit."

Carpe Diem — Seize the Day!

I woke up with a jolt. Our bedroom was already filled with morning sunlight.

"Oh no! What happened to the alarm! We've overslept." I couldn't believe it. "We're going to be late for work!"

I shook John's shoulder quickly as I jumped out of bed. He stretched, slowly opened his eyes, and gave me a mischievous grin.

"Come back to bed," he said. "I took the day off . . . don't worry, I also called your boss."

A free morning, an unscheduled afternoon, a day off in the middle of the week . . . sometimes the luxury of free time falls into your lap; sometimes you make it happen.

Add almond oil to some lotion, and offer an afternoon massage

•

Ask a professional masseuse to make a house call. Why not?

•

Curl up and nap together . . . and then take a long soak . . . mix in some bubbles, some fragrance, and make room for two

•

Order out . . . from your favorite restaurant. Yes, they'll do it . . . just ask

•

Shower together . . . and wash each other's hair

•

Stay up late . . . then sleep in

•

Snuggle . . . just snuggle

•

Sit and sip . . . on the sofa, on the porch steps

Couples told us how romantic they feel when they claim these days as special time for just themselves. Freed from the phone, routine, schedules, and those "gotta do's," they retreat from the world and concentrate on each other. They take time to appreciate being together; to pamper each other or to happily putter about. They share a project or share a nap.

Or they seize that free time and run with it. Explore new places. Play tourist in their own town. Refresh themselves with an afternoon swim. Or get away to the nearest mountaintop.

As one two-career couple said, "Whatever we do, free time together is like a tonic. The break in the routine and the uninterrupted focus on each other leaves us glowing, feeling close, and refreshed."

To make the most of it, plan for it. Savor the anticipation. Even talking about your fantasy day is exciting. And, as a number of couples advised, it's a good idea to have a plan or two in reserve for when you get an unexpected gift of time. That's when you can truly Seize the Day!

HEART IS WHERE THE HOME IS . . .

There are delightful ways to spend time together just around the house. A cup of tea together in bed, a card game, a video on a rainy day, or breakfast on a sunny deck . . . unplug the phone, turn on the answering machine . . . quiet time at home can be that simple. Just sitting together, "him watching a ballgame, me doing a crossword puzzle," is cozy contentment.

"Occasionally we tell our friends that we're going away, and then stay home undisturbed. We make a special brunch together, have a glass of wine, play soft music, massage each other, take a nap. Then we have dinner at one of our favorite quiet spots." After a day like this, both go back to their normal daily routines feeling relaxed and very close to each other.

FUN WITH FOOD

*Roast marshmallows,
chestnuts, popcorn . . .
in the fireplace*

•

*Bake a batch of your
favorite cookies . . .
and share the bowl of
leftover cookie dough*

•

*Linger over a very,
very long brunch*

•

*Breakfast in bed, in the
garden, at the park*

•

Picnic on the back lawn

•

*Dine by candlelight
with cloth napkins
and a tablecloth . . .
outdoors*

∽

Small Investment — Big Return

Five years ago . . .

We were in the housewares department trying to match a broken cup when we saw it. "It's so romantic," I said.

"But on our budget, isn't it kind of an indulgence?" he asked.

"It's on sale," I pointed out, "and we can use it to bring in soup if one of us is sick." We can rationalize almost anything.

◆

Today . . .

We've repainted our breakfast tray twice, because we use it so much (yes, once when I was sick, he did actually bring me soup on it).

Early Sunday mornings we can hear the birds chirping. We wake up very slowly to the sun streaming in through the window. We can smell the coffee brewing downstairs (it's set on a timer). One of us brings in the morning paper, the other the tray with coffee, and it's back to bed for a lazy morning together.

Recently we've started to recapture some of that Sunday magic during the week. We often set our alarms a half hour earlier to create extra time together in bed with our tray of coffee . . . and what do you know? — the birds chirp during the week too!

Reading together can be an entertaining and relaxing activity. You may have childhood memories of having the Sunday comics read to you, or a chapter of your favorite book when you were tucked into bed. Even though you're grown up, you can enjoy this . . . with a new twist. Exploring new ideas together, stimulating your imaginations, sharing a chuckle—reading together can be pure enjoyment.

"When we have time off, sometimes we just sit and listen to music, sip coffee, read, and talk about what we're reading. We read the interesting parts out loud to each other."

Magazines, newspapers, books . . . during breakfast . . . before dinner . . . on a lazy Sunday afternoon . . . romantic poetry at bedtime—couples often mentioned how they use reading to create special time.

LEARN SOMETHING NEW TOGETHER

Listen to language tapes . . . and rent a movie in your new language • Buy two fresh notebooks, sharpen your pencils, and take a course offered on public television • Learn a new skill from a "how-to" video or audio tape . . . building benches or building muscles . . . • Attend a home improvement fair and take a seminar on . . . wallpapering, sprinkler systems, woodworking . . . • Take your old dog to learn new tricks . . . in an obedience class • Learn to play a musical instrument together . . . toot recorders, strum guitars

READING
TOGETHER

*Film history . . . rent
films to go along with it*

•

*Drama . . . read
and act out the plays*

•

*History . . .
of your town,
of your region . . .
and go visit the sites*

•

*Art . . . include some
visits to museums
and galleries*

•

*Magazine articles . . .
share your common
interests or your
individual ones*

•

*Erotica . . . share
your common interests*

Who Dunnit

During a howling storm, with a crash of thunder, our power went off. There we sat in pitch blackness. We could see each other only during the brilliant silver flashes of lightning. The wind was thrashing the branches of the elm tree that towers over our house, threatening to bring them down. As the thunder rolled and rumbled, rain and hail pelted the windows.

She lit the storm candles and set them around the room. Then, without a word, she went to the bookcase, selected a book, sat down, and opened it to the first page.

Her voice took on an ominous and foreboding tone as she began to read from *Dracula*. I literally felt goosebumps. I could almost hear the creak of the coffin opening . . . just as Dracula was about to speak, she handed me the book to continue reading.

Since then, we've continued to read ghost and mystery stories to each other. It's become one of our favorite things to do, even if the weather doesn't always provide the special effects it did that first night.

But couples also find that special time together is not limited to leisure activities. Even routine chores can be romantic, if they draw you closer together. You can find tremendous satisfaction in "finally getting to" that project that keeps getting bumped down the list. And doing it together can leave you feeling close. Sometimes doing the chore together turns out to be more fun than you would have guessed.

Wash Me

Embarrassing, but we finally got the message. Someone had written "Wash Me" in the dust on our car. To be honest, the yard didn't look all that well-kept either — the weeds were threatening to take over. We'd been putting it off too long. So we set aside a Saturday just for the car and the yard.

I would tackle the garden; he would clean the car. The day was ideal — sunny and warm. We brought out the radio, tuned it to an oldies station and got started.

The timing was perfect. I was humming along to a Beach Boys surfing song when I felt the spray of water on my legs. He said, "Oops. It was just an accident." But his laughing gave him away. Well, two can play that game. I had a hose too, and when he turned around to clean the tires, I blasted him. That started it. By the time we stopped, we were both drenched and laughing so hard our sides hurt.

ROMANTIC CHORES

Dig into the garden . . . herbs, flowers, vegetables . . . build a fishpond, a gazebo, a sundeck

•

Consolidate the memories . . . put a photo album together, frame some pictures for a photo wall, label all those family videos

•

Two cooks in the kitchen . . . concoct an elaborate meal, try a new cuisine, make your own sausage, set up your own brewery

•

It's your dream house . . . paint it, tile it, add shelves to it

•

Wash that car, wash that dog

FOOLING AROUND TOWN

It's possible to spend your time off just around town and still feel you had a real getaway. An early evening walk or bike ride through a lovely old residential neighborhood, "looking for the perfect house," or comparing gardens, is simple and satisfying. "We love to pick a Dallas street, put on good walking shoes (and taxi fare in our pockets 'just in case'), then follow that street to its end."

Or hop in the car and go for an aimless drive. Along the way you might stumble on a real "find," an out-of-the-way antique store, a local farmers' market, a hubcap museum, or "the most beautiful old road in the world"—and sharing the discovery makes it all the better.

"God made the country and man made the town."
William Cowper

42

Get Lost

We love to go for drives in the countryside . . . we take a map, and my wife navigates. Or usually does. Once she deliberately tried to get us lost, just for the fun of finding our way out of it.

———◄►———

We were driving up the coast one afternoon when I told him to take a narrow side road. I didn't even know if it went through or dead-ended. It wound up into the hills full of pine trees, meadows, pastures, and a charming farm with geese and goats, and roses climbing on the barn. Each turn of the road seemed more beautiful than the last. We ended up in a tiny whistlestop where we had a great spaghetti dinner. To this day he calls this lane "our" road.

"Sunday is a day that clears away the rust of the week."
Joseph Addison

Many New Yorkers haven't been to the top of the Empire State Building, and many Missourians have never taken a steamboat ride on the Mississippi . . . why not play tourist in your own town? It can give you a fresh perspective, and you may discover places you didn't know existed!

Skeletons in Their Closets

When my sister and brother-in-law came to visit last month, they brought along a guidebook to the city. After they left, I was going to toss it when a quirky ad caught my eye. It was for a walking tour called "Skeletons in Their Closets."

This was a tour of the old mansions of the founding fathers of the city, with information about their not-so-civic pasts. It sounded so intriguing, we took the tour.

One of the homes was built for a mistress. Another home was built using embezzled funds. Another upright old family got its start by smuggling rum. Our city streets, named after these scoundrels, will never be the same to us!

Neighborhood Tourists

It was one of those gorgeous balmy spring days, not a cloud in the sky, with a light breeze blowing off the bay. The kind of day that makes you feel like running off and joining the circus. However, we were off to get groceries.

On the way to the market, we saw three tourists looking at a street map. They talked enthusiastically for a while and then strolled on. They looked so carefree, all smiles and eager chatter, that we both said how lucky they were to be tourists in our city. Then she said, "Why not us?" Why not indeed! The groceries could certainly wait until that evening. We became tourists for a day.

We explored a neighborhood we'd always meant to visit. We found an antique shop that specialized in toys — a wonderful red fire truck, mechanical piggy banks, a fifty-year-old tricycle, trains, and dolls of every size and shape. Down the street was a bookstore that must have had every travel guide ever written. We wandered into a café, got a window table, and indulged in espresso and Italian pastries while we people-watched. Then we moved on. Arm in arm we just strolled through the afternoon.

PLACES
AROUND
TOWN

Fairs . . .
County Fair,
Renaissance Faire,
craft fair

•

Parks . . .
amusement park,
theme park,
city park

•

Movies . . .
matinee,
retrospective, preview

•

Concerts . . .
local talent,
artist on tour,
outdoor, bandstand

•

Ballgames . . .
baseball, basketball,
football, bocce ball

•

Museums . . .
art, natural history,
antique cars,
baseball cards

When the free day or afternoon is not impromptu, and you have the luxury of planning ahead, you can prepare a more structured way to spend time together. Sports events, concerts, the theater . . . you can let your interests be your guide. And couples also told us how, for variety, they "plan" surprises now and then.

Fair Trade

When we first got married, all we could afford for a big night out was to go to a movie.

When I got home from work one night, I found an envelope hanging from the ceiling light in the middle of the kitchen. It had my name on it, in my wife's handwriting. I assumed my wife was creatively telling me to start dinner. I just couldn't believe it. Inside was a pair of tickets to the Rolling Stones concert!

Bob loved the Rolling Stones. He had every record they'd ever made. Not to mention two Stones' T-shirts. When they came on tour, I knew I had to get tickets by hook or by crook. I pinched and saved. Then I had to figure how to get the tickets — people were camping in line for them! I couldn't, because I had to go to work. But our teenage niece could. It cost me, though. I traded my sewing skills for her waiting-in-line skills and made her a skirt. Boy, was it worth it. I'll never forget the look of shock and then delight on his face when he saw those tickets.

Take Me Out to the Ballgame

"And it's one, two, three strikes you're out . . ."
To put it mildly, we are both ardent Braves fans,
and Atlanta is only an hour away. This year we
finally did what we've always wanted to do . . .
we got season tickets and haven't missed a single
home game.

We take turns driving . . . one of us there, the
other back. We've got such a case of baseball fever,
we've been reading baseball stories aloud in the
car. We've already read *Shoeless Joe*, and now we're
finishing *Boys of Summer*.

MOVING
AROUND
TOWN

*Walk . . . through the
park, through a
neighborhood, to the
end of a street*

•

*Walk to discover . . .
your dream house,
your dream garden*

•

*Walk to look at
the architecture*

•

*Fly . . .
in a small plane,
in a helicopter*

•

Café hop, people-watch

47

Physical activity—from a walk through the park to a strenuous afternoon of bike riding, tennis, or hiking—simply makes you feel good. In addition to the long-term health benefits, exercise leaves us energized, glowing, feeling upbeat. Few things equal its payback for the amount of time invested in it.

Add to that the pleasure of sharing it with your partner, and you have a powerful combination. No wonder so many couples exercise and play together. They walk, jog, toss a Frisbee,™ play tennis, dance . . . together.

A woman from Oregon told us, "My favorite romantic activity is bike riding together. I know, it may not seem romantic, but when we can share a physical activity, it seems to draw us closer. We take all kinds of rides together. It doesn't matter if it's an organized tour or just something we do on the spur of the moment. What's important is that we enjoy the exertion."

Cheek to Cheek

When there's music, I can't sit still. I'm a dancer. I've taken ballet, jazz, tap, ballroom, you name it. My husband, on the other hand, thinks of himself as someone with two left feet.

She can't sit down when the music starts, so I have to make some kind of effort. Fred Astaire doesn't have anything to worry about, but I can keep a beat. Used to tap it out with my fingers while I listened to music. She's teaching me to add my feet. Who knows . . . maybe the rest of my body will follow!

I started teaching him the Lindy and the Cha Cha on Sunday afternoons. We kid around about pulling down the shades so no one can see him dancing, but really, he's getting pretty good. And we love the energy we feel when we're dancing together.

GETTING CLOSE

Roll the rug back and dance to oldies in the living room

•

Watch movies in bed on a rainy day . . . a romantic film, a musical, something erotic, something silly . . .

•

Zip two sleeping bags together and rent a scary movie

•

Close the shades and read erotica to each other

•

Borrow or rent a video camera and create your own video . . . something funny, something that needs a rating . . .

MOVING TOGETHER

On the water . . .
sailing, canoeing, wind-
surfing, water skiing

•

In the air . . .
sky diving,
hang gliding,
bungee jumping

•

On the court . . .
tennis, volleyball,
handball

•

Hit the trails . . .
biking,
mountain biking,
cross-country skiing

•

Hit the floor . . .
dancing, working out

•

Hit the golf course
and swing

Take Your Partner

I'm eighty-two years old, and my wife and I have been married for fifty-five years. And I'd have to say that the last twenty-two years have been the best since the two of us took up square dancing.

Every Tuesday and Friday night we dress up and go square dancing downtown at the community center. Four times a year we go to square dancing conventions all over the Southeast, where we dance at events that are held all day long. We've even gone across the country to attend national dances and have met wonderful and interesting people everywhere we've gone.

The dances are more than just vigorously moving about the floor in swinging circles . . . the fun starts at home when we dress for each event, usually wearing something matching. I'll put on a yellow shirt and bolo tie; my wife ties on a yellow scarf, and under her yellow plaid skirt, she has on several crinolines and yellow lacy pants.

Over the years, we've learned to dance at the highest levels, Advanced II . . . with the caller barking tricky commands faster and faster. And the more we do it, the more we enjoy it, and the stronger we feel.

If It's Volleyball, It Must Be Tuesday

While there may not be a gold medal in our future, we both love to play volleyball. We belong to a group that meets every Tuesday evening after work. We have a standing order with our baby-sitter for those evenings. And, interestingly, even though we're playing with a lot of other people, we really feel like these are special evenings out for us. We come home physically tired, but emotionally high as a kite.

"If I had known I was going to live this long, I would have taken better care of myself."
Unknown

Be Prepared

The Boy Scout motto has not been lost on us! We love to play golf together. We have an agreement: whatever else goes into the trunk of our car, there's always room for our clubs. And when the chance comes to putt around, we're ready to go.

If we can get home from work earlier than usual, we head for the golf course and play as long as the light permits. We follow this with dinner out. This may not sound "sexy," but we spend so many hours working that when we can take the time to share something we both enjoy, believe me, it's romantic.

THE WONDERFUL OUTDOORS

"We need the tonic of . . . nature."
Henry David Thoreau

Couples repeatedly talked about how romantic it is to watch the sunrise, the sunset, the full moon, or the tiniest sliver of a silvery crescent moon. They described being at an isolated lake, swimming in the fresh cold water. Or sitting together on a hillside of fragrant green grass. The feeling of quiet contentment and marvel is one that can be shared, and enjoyed, even without speaking.

Everyone has their way of getting back in touch with nature. Walking together, riding bikes, riding horses, swimming, windsurfing . . . and picnics. Picnics in the park. Picnics at the beach. Picnics in the desert when the spring flowers start blooming. It only takes a special place where the world doesn't intrude, even your own back yard.

Stargazers

Sometimes, on a summer evening, we take our porch chairs down to the garden to watch the last of the sunset. As it gets dark, the stars begin to come out one by one, and suddenly there are more than you can count. We have a cup of tea and just stargaze. We don't say much. Just hold hands.

Light Show

We were on vacation in Michigan. Without city lights to drown them out, the night sky looked like a sea of stars. We bought a constellation guide and every night we tried to identify a few more. And, although most configurations looked the same to me, with our heads close and our arms around each other, it didn't matter if the Big Dipper looked like a bear or an old saucepan. Then one night it happened. The Northern Lights burst across the sky. I'd never seen them before — it was a stunning sight. Whenever I see stars I think of those nights, and the feeling of being close comes rushing back.

BEING CREATIVE TOGETHER

Take up photography, build a darkroom in your basement (just big enough for two)

•

Make your Christmas presents throughout the year . . . wreaths, preserves, painted boxes, bookends . . .

•

Draw with neon paints, pastels, oils . . . or paint by numbers

•

Sing . . . Folk songs, church choir, just for each other

Beachcombers

We are fortunate to live within a half-mile of the ocean. We make a special effort to get to the beach as often as we can. A walk after work is a bracing tonic. We take our shoes off and stroll along the water line, where the sand is firm and wet. Fantasies of quitting work and becoming beach bums occasionally enter the conversation. But the cold water splashing over our ankles is enough to wake us up. For some it may be meditating, for others a workout, but for us, a walk on the beach is how we wash away the pressures of the workday.

"There is no pleasure in having nothing to do; the fun is having lots to do and not doing it."

John W. Raper

54

Gone Fishing

I'd gone fishing now and then, and it was O.K., but my girlfriend grew up in a fishing family. Her dad's specialty was fly-fishing, and eventually he taught her brothers how to cast. She'd always been sorry she'd never learned, too. So when there was a fly-fishing course offered at the community center, I said I'd go along with her, sort of for moral support.

It turns out when they talk about fly-fishing class they really mean half fly-fishing and half learning how to tie flies. She became a real whiz at tying flies. I didn't care so much for that, but I got so I could catch a trout or two with a fly. Now when we go out, she ties whatever they're biting. She ties for both of us, but she strikes a hard bargain: she makes me clean whatever we catch. We've spent some wonderful times fishing (and eating) together.

Away from It All in Boston

Lush greenery, trees, small animals rustling in the underbrush, the air filled with bird songs. It would be easy to forget we were in the heart of Boston, and not on our fantasy trip in a Montana wilderness.

For a lot of people this is a place for sports, jogging, and walking . . . for some the sunny park benches are a peaceful place to sit and people-watch . . . but for us this park is a place to get away from the city. We bring a blanket to lounge on and a picnic basket full of goodies . . . it's "our" special retreat.

"Why are there trees I never walk under, but large and melodious thoughts descend upon me?"
Walt Whitman

Healing Plants

My husband works for the Forest Service and spends most of his time outdoors. He has a passion for it. So it was double trouble when he took a bad fall and found himself with his leg strung up in traction, immobile. Cooped up, couldn't go out, couldn't do anything that he loved to do. He was getting really down about it all.

So one day I surprised him. While he was asleep, I quietly brought in all my potted plants from the deck. While I was lugging in the fan to create a breeze, he woke up. He was astonished. Then I laid out a picnic lunch on a blanket in the middle of the bed.

I woke up all ready to complain about the racket she was making when I saw what she was up to. What a nice thing to do for me! The place looked like a jungle. (A weird jungle—when would you see a cactus next to an azalea! I like to give her a hard time about that.) She sure brought the outdoors in for me.

BEING
CREATIVE
TOGETHER

Write . . . poetry, limericks, children's stories, a journal

•

Make puppets and create a puppet show . . . traditional or off-beat

•

Build furniture . . . a rocking chair, porch swing, bookcase

•

Volunteer your time for a cause important to both of you

Romance and the Senses

The senses give texture and substance to our experiences. Senses shape our attitudes, inform our perceptions, and add dimension to our relationships. They're how we continually acquire the myriad details that we absorb from the world around us.

The distant, gentle tinkling of a piano heard through an open window on a balmy night, the softness of a cashmere sweater against a cheek during a returning home embrace, the pungent smell of a wood fire and hot smoky peppers in a tangy salsa on a beach in Mexico, the squeaky crunch of footsteps on newly fallen snow, the sun spreading bars of golden light through a louvered shutter . . . all of these can be acutely felt sensations of touch, taste, smell, sound, and sight . . . when we pay attention to them.

"We are astonished at thought but sensation is equally wonderful."
Voltaire

LIGHT, LOVELY LIGHT

Candles . . .
a forest of them,
in candlesticks,
candelabras,
on candle stands,
in votive glasses . . .
in many colors
or all one . . .
fragrant, with floral,
herbal, exotic scents

•

Colored light . . .
a pink light bulb for a
soft, inviting light . . .
magenta paint on a
plain low-wattage bulb
to create just the
right glow

•

Firelight . . .
campfires,
fireplace glow

•

Low light . . .
oil lamps,
lower wattage bulbs,
dimmers, night-lights

•

Filtered sun . . .
through louvers,
through shutters,
through the trees

The senses combine and reinforce one another, enriching our lives. When we take the time to find or create an environment that is especially lovely or particularly romantic, the sensory experience is heightened. So many couples talked about how they orchestrate their environments to shape and embellish their experiences.

SIGHT

Beauty arrests us. We stop and gaze at a richly hued sunset, taking it in completely until the last pale color fades to gray. We catch our breath at the silver luminescence of the full moon, or at the rich gold of the

60

harvest moon. The sight of the sun's rays filtering through the dense trees and dust motes of a forest glade remains etched in memory for years.

Nothing transforms the environment like light. The bright white lights of a busy work area . . . the intensely focused cone of light on a book . . . the softly diffused yellow light of a candle . . . the glow of a sunset—each influences us in different ways. We instinctively speak more quietly, softly, in a candle-lit room.

The candle is probably the simplest and most powerful way to create a romantic ambience. A single candle can transform the most ordinary room into a mysterious or peaceful retreat.

Bathed in Light

One of the most relaxing things I do for myself is to take a bath, and let the cares of the world drift away.

One evening, while dreamily immersed in lemon-scented luxury, I found myself thinking about my husband and how tense he had been over some problems at work. I thought, "A relaxing bath like this would do wonders for him."

I began to envision how I could transform this functional bathroom into a sanctuary for him. I'd have to clear away the toothpaste tubes, the dental floss, the contact lens solution bottles . . . all the stuff that clutters the room.

"The eyes are the window of the soul."
Proverb

SAVORING
THE BATH

*Flowers . . .
arranged in vases,
growing in pots . . .
fragrant lilies,
the elegance of
blooming orchids*

•

Candles

•

Body paint

•

*A rubber duck . . .
a toy boat*

SAVORING
THE BATH

*The thickest, softest
terry towels and
washcloths you can find*

•

*A plush terry robe . . .
a silky robe . . .
a light, cotton robe*

•

*A new scrub brush . . .
big, fluffy, natural
sponges . . . a loofah*

•

*Lotions, bubble bath,
bath gel, bath oil,
fragrances . . .
in pretty jars
and bottles*

•

*Soap . . . big bars,
pretty shapes,
fragrant with floral
or herbal scents*

•

*Baskets, decorative
boxes and bottles . . .
to hide the everyday
necessities of the
bathroom*

One Saturday morning my wife said sweetly, "Honey, I've got a special treat for you tonight. Please put on the new robe I gave you for your birthday and meet me outside the bathroom at 7 P.M." I nearly choked on my English muffin. But it did sound intriguing.

So there I was, on time, standing outside the bathroom door, fiddling with the belt on my robe. At exactly 7, she opened the door.

Instead of the usual bright light, the bathroom was lit by a lot of flickering candles. There were colorful flowers on the counter next to the sink, and all the usual stuff that fills the room was gone. On a little table next to the tub (she had made it by throwing a piece of cloth over a step stool!), there were two glasses of wine and some small jars and bottles of lotions. The room smelled good. To top it off, there was harp music coming from a portable tape player. But the candles — on the tub, on the sink, on the shelves — were what really made the room sexy and inviting.

I'd never had an experience like this — I usually take showers. She scrubbed my back and massaged my shoulders. She rubbed my feet. She even washed my hair. I never knew there could be so much pleasure in taking a bath. I said, "I'll do this for you," but she told me to forget about that now, just to sit back and enjoy.

The Blooming of the Sunrise

When we were on vacation in a remote part of Belize, we found our internal clock changed. There were no phones, radio, or TV. We usually finished dinner shortly after sunset, and then sat on the deck to watch the stars before turning in.

Each morning we'd wake up earlier and earlier, until finally, one morning, we were awake at 5 A.M., long before sunrise. As soon as the hotel's generator went on, we made a small pot of strong coffee and sat outside watching the sunrise slowly unfold.

The sky was profoundly beautiful as it gradually grew lighter; the wispy clouds and the sea were tinged in shades of pink. Birds began to stir; a phalanx of pelicans swept by, dark gray in the growing light. The soft, glowing sunrise had bloomed into the full glory of a sunny tropical morning.

We were so moved by the experience, such a rich way to start the day, that we promised ourselves we'd continue doing this when we returned home.

For the most part we have, although it takes more effort than it did when we were on vacation. But we've started going to bed earlier, and we usually get up before sunrise. In the summer, we sit with our coffee in the backyard, and in the winter, by the kitchen window.

LIGHT,
LOVELY
LIGHT

Sunrise, sunsets . . .
on the beach,
in the desert,
from a ship,
from a mountaintop

•

Sunshine . . .
moonshine . . .
starshine

•

Absence of light . . .
a moonless night . . .
a power outage
during a storm

•

Light as color

"Sight—the
keenest of all of
our senses."
Cicero

TOUCH

Deprive us of touch and we literally lose contact with our world. The sense of touch is a powerful source of information about our environment. We can't help but reach out with pleasure to touch an enticing surface: the satin softness of a baby's skin, the smoothness of polished wood, the rich shimmer of silk, the froth of bath bubbles.

You can surround yourselves with tactile riches . . . choose sensuous bedding, downy soft pillows, comfortable silky loungewear, the thickest towels.

"The (romantic) embrace can only be compared with music and with prayer."

Havelock Ellis

64

Touching each other—holding hands, caressing, stroking one another—one couple called this a "gift" they give each other. And if a massage feels good to a tired back, if it's such a relief for sore muscles to be rubbed with ointments, think of the pleasure of having oils and lotions massaged into muscles that are not sore or tired.

Touching Toes

For my birthday, my best friend gave me a gift certificate for a professional beauty treatment that included a facial, a manicure, and a pedicure. The first two were nothing new to me, but I had never had a pedicure; I had no idea that it included a foot massage. What a magical treatment! It's amazing how relaxing it can be just to have your feet pressed and kneaded with fragrant lotions.

The experience made a convert of me. I bought some oils and lotions, and tried what I'd learned on my husband. He enjoyed it so much that we bought a book on massage techniques, and now we take turns giving each other full massages. We've learned not to massage each other on the same evening: each of us is much too relaxed afterward to even think of reciprocating!

*Sensuous clothing . . .
satins, silks . . . fresh,
soft cotton . . .*

•

*Towels . . .
thick and soft . . .
warmed by the
clothes dryer*

•

*Warmed oils,
cool powders*

•

*Bedding . . .
fresh sheets,
piles of pillows,
soft blankets*

•

*Furniture . . .
the softest couch . . .
thick throw pillows . . .
inviting fabrics*

•

*Massage . . . the back,
the face, the scalp,
the feet and hands . . .
with oils and lotions,
a fur mitt*

•

*Cuddle . . . hold hands,
hug, hold each other*

•

*Slow dancing . . .
cheek to cheek*

SCENT

SCENT, AROMA, FRAGRANCE

Nature . . . damp earth after a rain . . . newly mown grass, hay . . . ocean spray and seaweed . . . a pine forest

•

Food . . . freshly baked bread . . . hot popcorn . . . anything with cinnamon

C lose your eyes, think about an aroma you enjoy, and you can find yourself transported to another place. The fragrance of honeysuckle . . . the back porch of your childhood home. The sweet smell of vanilla . . . the kitchen of a close friend. The rich aroma of hot chocolate . . . that winter vacation in the mountains. The fragrance of baby oil . . . your college days, on a beach during spring break. Scent carries such strong associations that it can easily bring to mind even long-forgotten memories.

Most people are aware that without scent we have very little taste. But scent is so powerful that it also deeply affects the other senses. When a significant aroma causes you to recall an experience, you not only remember it visually, but you also hear its sounds, and feel the environment.

"Nothing awakens a reminiscence like a (scent)."
Victor Hugo

The Call of the Islands

On a trip to Hawaii, our first impression — the strongest one — was the scents of all the tropical flowers. We reveled in the sensuousness of the fragrances, especially the plumeria leis we wore around our necks.

Now, when we bring flowers into the house, I try to select those with the strongest aromas. Sometimes we even string them around our necks like leis. The wonderful, pungent aromas bring back the feeling and mood of Hawaii — a real aphrodisiac.

Petal Magic

For our fifteenth wedding anniversary celebration, he told me he had something special planned. All I had to do was "join the festivities" in the den.

I hardly recognized the room. There were over thirty candles, in different shapes and sizes, spread everywhere. The dark wood of the furniture glowed in the light, and shadows danced everywhere. Quiet flute music played in the background. In the middle of the floor he had arranged an inviting mound of soft pillows and blankets. But the most extraordinary thing about the room was the scent: the strong fragrance of roses. He'd bought a huge bag of rose petals at the flower mart and sprinkled them all over our romantic setting!

SCENT,
AROMA,
FRAGRANCE

*Fresh flowers . . . roses,
lilies, freesias,
jasmine, stock,
honeysuckle, lilacs,
gardenias, violets*

•

*Florals . . .
essential oils,
potpourri*

•

*Herbals . . . rosemary,
lavender, mint*

•

*Spicy . . . nutmeg,
ginger, clove, vanilla*

•

*Fruity . . . orange,
lemon, lime,
apricot, apple*

•

Exotic incense

•

*Perfumed . . . cologne,
perfume, scented
candles, fragrant bath
salts, scented soaps*

TRANSFORMING YOUR ENVIRONMENT WITH SOUND

*Music . . . whatever
kind makes you feel
peaceful, romantic,
loving, contemplative,
cheerful . . .
or like dancing*

•

*Nature's sounds . . .
the ocean, the river,
the forest, the rain,
the wind, the birds*

•

*Voice . . . recordings of
someone singing,
reading, talking*

*"If music be
the food of love,
play on . . ."*
Shakespeare

Listen . . . What do you hear? Rustling trees, perhaps . . . a mockingbird . . . the rain . . . someone hammering . . . the hum of traffic . . . children playing . . . a radio or TV . . . a washing machine. We hear such a range of sounds each day and they often elicit strong emotions.

Some of these are a joy; others you would rather do without. With sound you can create your own environment. If you live with distracting outside noises, you can displace them with music and change your environment. You can create a lively atmosphere or a quiet, peaceful sanctuary. With the appropriate music you can reinforce or change a mood, a feeling, an attitude.

Music is a powerful, emotional force. From religious hymns that inspire spirituality to martial music that stimulates patriotism, music has long been used to shape and define what we feel. Music can express rollicking fun, intense longing, or rapturous romance — and carry the listener right along with these feelings.

Almost universally, couples gave us descriptions of the music they use to transform their moods. When they're feeling tired and irritable, music is soothing. When they need a lift, the right music picks them up. One couple, from New York, talked about their winter music "prescription"—"On a dull, gray day, sometimes we'll put on our old rock and roll records. They're so cheerful, they make us feel great. We sing right along; our kids think we're nuts."

Another couple feels close when they listen to Neil Diamond. For a third it's Puccini's operas. For each couple, the delight is not only in the music, but in sharing something they love.

Every couple has "our song"—and often it's the first dance at their wedding reception or it's associated with a special occasion or feeling. It's something that unites a couple and brings smiles to their faces from the moment they hear the first few bars.

"Everybody should have his personal sounds to listen for—sounds that make him exhilarated and alive or quiet and calm."
André Kostelanetz

*"The song that we
hear with our ears
is only the song
that is sung in
our hearts."*
Ouida

*"Those who wish
to sing always
find a song."*
Swedish proverb

Our Song

When we were first dating, we lived near the
Southern California coast. Of course we spent a
lot of time at the beach. Bikinis were just coming
into vogue, and I had one of the first. About that
time a very silly song came out: "Itsy Bitsy Teeny
Weeny Yellow Polka Dot Bikini." Plenty of songs
from that era were far more romantic, but that
one became "our song." Other people raise their
eyebrows—they think we're crazy—but that song
means a lot to us. For us it represents those early
days when we first fell in love.

Meals, too, can be transformed by music—plain "eating" becomes "dining" when you change the atmosphere by playing whatever music you find romantic.

TASTE

Taste is influenced by all of the other senses. The most dramatic illustration of this is how a mundane meal can be changed into a splendid dining experience.

Food is such an important part of romance . . . the allure of a dimly lit restaurant, the enchantment of a picnic, the romance of a table by the fireplace, the sensuousness of luscious foods, the power of wonderful aromas, the lure of aphrodisiacs . . . food is so romantic that it belongs in a chapter by itself.

Sensuous Meals

One Sunday morning we took a walk through Coconut Grove, an old, picturesque section of Miami. We love watching the tall palm trees on both sides of the street sway gently in the soft tropical breeze. We slowly browsed through a few art galleries before heading to our favorite café. We chose an outdoor table for two tucked among the hibiscus and azalea, with a view of the street.

Our order: two bowls of fresh, long-stemmed strawberries, a small bowl of melted chocolate for dipping, and a cold bottle of champagne in a silver ice bucket.

We giggled like school kids as we slowly fed the dripping chocolate berries to each other, giddy with the awareness that the other patrons were gawking at us. We felt like we were in the movies, only this was far more delicious.

"Food — the first enjoyment of life."
Lin Yu Tang

Food is far more than mere fuel for our bodies — the satisfaction experienced from those strawberries and chocolate had very little to do with physical hunger.

Food can stimulate or relax, nurture or seduce. Food can be very traditional or highly experimental. Food can act — or seem to act — as an aphrodisiac. It can be the focus of an activity; other times it's a perfect complement to another activity.

And we don't just taste food; we savor it with all our other senses as well. We use our sense of smell; without it, we'd be limited to the four simple distinctions of salty, sweet, bitter, and sour, hardly the sensory range we use to enjoy a hot fudge sundae. We also use our sense of touch — to appreciate the cracking crust on a piece of French bread, to roll a creamy bite of Brie cheese over our tongue, to feel a piece of milk chocolate melt in our mouth.

Light and color also influence the appeal of food. Even our sense of hearing comes into play: the sizzle of a grilling steak makes our mouth water in anticipation, and the crunch of a breakfast cereal is so important that manufacturers sell it as a "benefit."

Food can also be part of our reminiscences: some couples cherish certain foods just because they are "their" foods. One couple described how they periodically stop for Chinese take-out on the way home from work and eat their double order of potstickers in the car. They laugh about how they never get the potstickers home.

Another couple bought matching hand-painted dishes when they were dating, and for years have been enjoying desserts on "their" dishes.

While individual tastes in food run the gamut (what makes one person's mouth water makes another's nose wrinkle), for all of us, the ambience surrounding the food makes a world of difference. A peanut butter sandwich eaten hastily at your desk tastes different from the one you leisurely enjoy while lounging on a blanket next to a running stream. Orange juice you gulp while standing in front of the open refrigerator tastes different from the juice sipped from a monogrammed glass ordered through room service at a resort hotel.

Whether they had recently begun dating or were together for many years, couples all agreed that food plays an important role in bringing people together—from dinner with friends to an elaborate party. It's also the planning, shopping, and preparing that present other opportunities to do something enjoyable and romantic together.

By being aware of how food and environment influence each other, it's possible for you to arrange settings that will enhance your meals and your life. Whether you are planning a picnic, a surprise meal, or a formal evening out, you can be as romantic as you want by creating the environment that makes your shared meal the special event you want it to be.

"The art of dining well is no slight art, The pleasure not a slight pleasure."
Montaigne

Picnics—everybody loves them! When we asked about memorable meals, virtually every questionnaire or comment came back describing a picnic. Some are extravagant, with a fancy presentation and haute cuisine; others are just as enjoyable when simple and inexpensive. Picnics are lovely in a traditional setting, such as a park, but many people love to think of unusual settings, such as in the snow, on a rooftop, or in their living room or bedroom. What picnics have in common is a sense of fun, of play, and of something different from our everyday mealtime routines.

Wonderland

Every year I try to think of something new for Valentine's Day. For us, something a bit offbeat is the stuff of romantic memories. Last year's will be hard to top.

On Valentine's morning, I packed a picnic basket with sparkling wine, cheeses, French bread, two little cherry tarts, and a thermos of hot coffee. I loaded our four-wheel-drive with warm blankets, and my wife and I took off for the snow-covered mountains.

We found a place where we could park near the road. Then we tramped a quarter mile through the snow to a clearing by a frozen brook. The only sounds were the distant babble of water running underneath the ice, the occasional "whoosh" of snow falling off a branch, and the raucous greeting of a curious blue jay. We spread out a tarp and some blankets, stuck the wine bottle in the snow, and set out our picnic.

There, in the frozen wonderland, we ate, drank, and were merry. And we had no problem keeping warm!

PICNICS, PICNICS EVERYWHERE

Under the stars

•

In a city plaza

•

In a public garden

•

By a country lane

•

At an outdoor concert

•

At a sporting event

•

On the highest hill

•

On a riverbank

•

On a ferryboat

•

In a rowboat

•

*In a pasture
(but be aware:
cows are very curious)*

IN THE PICNIC BASKET

*Keep a lovely old basket
always packed, handy,
and ready to go . . .
with flatware, napkins,
condiments,
a citronella candle
(to keep mosquitoes
at bay),
and a blanket.*

•

ADD TO THAT:
*Your favorite
take-out food*

•

*Cheeses . . . aged,
fresh, creamy, herb*

•

*Meats . . . sliced,
smoked, cured,
sausages, pâté*

•

*Breads . . . fresh rolls,
baguettes, croissants,
rye, nutty whole grain,
focaccia, pita, crackers*

Parking Lot Picnic

I'd had a difficult day. Being a nurse can be very stressful any time, but on that day my concern for a seriously ill patient, combined with the usual work demands, left me feeling drained.

My husband picked me up outside the emergency room entrance, and without my saying a word, he sensed I was really wrung out.

After we drove for a while in silence, I realized we were not on our way home. I asked where we were going. He smiled, said he knew that this wasn't the way home, and kept on driving.

We ended up in our old neighborhood. We had moved from there only six months before, and we still missed it. He parked in "our" shopping center and said he would be back in a few minutes. I was just to relax.

He seemed to take forever, and I was becoming irritated. But before my anger could build up, his face was smiling at me through the window.

He got into the car and handed me a bunch of pink tulips — my favorite flower. Then he produced a small Hawaiian pizza from "our" pizza shop. It's my favorite, but one he doesn't care for — that really touched me.

We sat in the car, shared the pizza, and talked about how we missed our old neighborhood. By the time the last piece of pizza was gone, so were the problems of my day.

On the Road

We've eaten in lots of restaurants and subscribe
to many of the food magazines. But when I think
of memorable meals, I think first of the time my
girlfriend and I were driving back to Phoenix
from Los Angeles. Just when our stomachs began
growling with hunger, the sky opened up with
a deluge — not a welcome sight to some, but to
those of us who live in the desert, it was beautiful
indeed. As we drove through the pouring rain
we could see a red neon light flashing the words
"Hickory-Smoked Bar-B-Que."

It sounded perfect, but the place was crowded
and noisy. So we had a picnic in the car. I turned
on the radio and found a good country & western
station. As we fed each other ribs and corn-on-the-
cob, we listened to Willie Nelson singing a duet
with the rain on the windshield.

Ebelskivers

He mailed me a card with the date and time he would pick me up, and a list of items I'd need: hiking shoes, swimsuit, camera — I was completely mystified. When he arrived, I asked where we were going, but all he would say was, "Do you like *ebelskivers*?"

Well, we ended up in a Danish village not far from Los Angeles. It was such a touristy thing to do that I had to laugh. But ten minutes later we were driving carts around the village. Then we took a short hike up to a nearby mountain lake.

By this time I was getting very hungry. A wonderful picnic spread appeared out of his backpack, as if by magic. In addition to the pastries we bought in town (including *ebelskivers*, which turned out to be a Danish goodie similar to an apple popover), there was smoked ham, Jarlsberg cheese, rolls, buttery pears, small crisp apples, and Danish beer.

Every time I think about *ebelskivers*, I recall . . .

"As life's pleasures go,
food is secondary only to sex.
Except for salami and eggs.
Now that's better than sex,
but only if the salami is thickly sliced."

Alan King

IN THE PICNIC
BASKET

Fruits . . . grapes,
apples, pears, cherries,
figs, oranges

•

Vegetables . . .
sliced carrots,
cucumber,
cherry tomatoes,
mushrooms,
raw cauliflower,
endive, radicchio . . .
with salsa,
with vinaigrette,
with dip

High-Rise Surprise

Once, on my day off, I called a co-worker at my husband's office and asked her to peek at his calendar to see if he'd be there during lunchtime. Sure enough, he was, so I packed a picnic, complete with red-checked cloth and napkins, sandwiches, juice, and various other tidbits. Then I took the commuter train into the city. When I surprised him at his office, he was astonished and delighted. We spread our picnic on the steps of a small sunny plaza next to his office building. There was something charming about bringing a picnic basket to his world of the attaché case!

———

A different kind of picnic requires "foraging" for the food. Pack a skillet on a fishing trip, for instance, make a campfire on the riverbank, and cook up the fresh trout right there on the spot: all you need is a lemon to squeeze over the fish and a few accompaniments for a perfect alfresco meal.

One couple told us about rising early in the morning on their vacation to go out berry picking, then returning to make blueberry pancakes for breakfast. Another wrote of visiting a small town built around a lovely grassy square. They strolled from shop to shop around the square, exploring the bakeries and interesting food shops, until they'd accumulated a delightful picnic lunch, which they enjoyed sitting on the grass.

IN THE PICNIC
BASKET

*Salads . . . coleslaw,
potato, pasta,
bean, fruit,
chicken, seafood*

•

*Other morsels . . .
roasted peppers,
marinated mushrooms,
marinated olives,
pickles, gherkins*

•

*Chips . . .
with salsa,
with dip*

•

*Bottles . . .
of sparkling water,
wine, beer, fruit juices,
soft drinks*

•

*Desserts . . . cookies,
cake, tarts, pastries*

•

*A Thermos™ . . . of
coffee, tea, iced tea*

TRANSFORMING
EATING INTO
DINING

SET OUT THE . . .
*Tablecloth or
attractive place mats*

·

Cloth napkins

·

*Best glassware,
nicest plates*

·

*Candles at night . . .
on stands,
in candlesticks*

·

*Condiments . . .
in serving dishes*

·

*Centerpiece . . .
a vase of flowers,
a bowl of fruit,
a bowl of pine cones,
a branch of
autumn leaves*

Dining (as distinguished from eating) at home sometimes gets lost amid everyone's busy and conflicting schedules. To prevent this, some couples make a point of always having dinner at the same time and reserving that time for each other. Others "celebrate" the weekend by making their Friday and/or Saturday evening dinners special. Some couples "dress" for dinner — a formality that adds to the pleasure of dining. Couples with small children sometimes create late, intimate dinners by feeding the children earlier and putting them to bed so the parents can dine peacefully alone.

Candles and Charred Pasta

We fed the kids and tucked them in a little earlier than usual so it would be just the two of us for dinner. Then we started assembling our Italian dinner: I made the meatballs and began the sauce while my wife put the salad together and the bread in the oven. While the sauce was simmering, I kissed her gently on the back of her neck . . . it would be foolish not to take advantage of the privacy. Well, yes, our dinner burned. But the candlelight setting was lovely for the pizza we ordered!

Even a family dinner with children can be dining with just a little effort.

Place Settings

We have three children, and without some "guidance," meals could easily get out of hand. Dinner should be pleasant, instead of an ordeal, so we decided to make some changes.

Now we dine — not just eat — and everyone contributes. Our five-year-old sets the table; she picks out the tablecloth and selects the candles each evening (on special occasions she puts all ten of them out!). She also adds touches of her own; she loves the brass coasters and puts them on the table under the candlesticks. She gets the silverware more or less correctly placed, and she experiments with interesting napkin folds.

Our seven-year-old makes the salad, pours the water, helps her sister with the table, and picks the flowers for the centerpiece. If our garden has no blooms, she gets creative with leaves, grasses, or even bare branches.

Our ten-year-old son does his piano practicing at this time, so his job is to clear the table after the meal and to help with the dishes.

We put out the dog. We dim the lights and light the candles, put on quiet music, and sit down to a very pleasant time together. We have some rules: no TV, no reading at the table, and no "horsing around" (burping contests, for example, are not OK). We've found that the kids respond very well to this. They need reminders, of course, but this is how they learn. And dinner has truly become a special time.

TRANSFORMING EATING INTO DINING

PUT AWAY THE . . .
Jars of catsup and mustard

•

Newspaper

•

TV Guide

•

Used apron and dishtowels

•

Sesame Street place mats

•

Plastic tumblers

TURN OFF THE . . .
Television

•

Telephone

•

Noisy appliances

•

TURN ON THE . . .
Music

•

Conversation

FOOD AS A GIFT

When a grandmother goes overboard to put together an enormous feast for the family, she's giving a gift of love. When there's a treat in the refrigerator waiting for a child after school, a parent is showing his or her love. When one partner prepares a favorite dish or arranges for going out to a favorite place for dinner, he or she is saying to their partner, "I love you."

A Dollop of Love

Last week I had to work overtime and came home exhausted and edgy. I didn't have much to say to Susan, didn't eat much for dinner, and went right to bed.

I awakened the next morning to the smell of coffee coming from the other room. Susan walked in carrying a tray with Swedish pancakes, lots of fresh strawberries topped with a mound of whipped cream, and a carafe of freshly brewed coffee.

I appreciated her just letting me be Mr. Grumpy the night before, and doing something extra-special to cheer me up the next day.

Appreciation

Recently, I spent the day at my elderly grandmother's house helping her clean while my husband stayed home and took care of our four-year-old daughter. The cleaning took all day—my grandmother has a large house, and she had not been feeling well enough to keep it up. When I got home that evening, I was ready to drop. I usually make dinner, so on the way home I was half thinking about what I could rustle up. I walked in the door . . . and my husband handed me a glass of wine. He had made dinner—something that he doesn't do often, so it did not come easily! He put on soothing music, and he and our daughter set the table with candles and fresh flowers they'd picked in the garden.

Boy, did I need this gift. Why did he do it? He told me, "I just wanted to make sure you felt appreciated and knew how much I love you."

Many men are fine cooks, but because cooking is so often seen as a "woman's domain," some of our best cooking stories are about men who gave it their all with the best of romantic intentions.

Where's the Fire?

When we started dating, John invited me to dinner at his place. Of course, he had a very romantic evening planned—delicious food, cognac by the fire, soft music.

A friend had given him a recipe for a chicken dish, but when he put it all together in his casserole, it filled up to the top and spilled over. Undaunted, he popped it into the oven anyway.

Then he tried to light the fire in the fireplace. As we sat in front of the smoky, gasping, not-quite fire, I began to wonder at what point I should tell him that I knew how to get the fire started. At about that time, the chicken caught fire in the oven! When he went to put out that fire, I quickly and quietly got the fire going in the fireplace. We had to laugh about how he intended to impress me, and how he got it all wrong about where to make the fire!

DINING OUT

When it comes to celebrating virtually anything, almost everyone talks about going out to a restaurant. It's her birthday? Go out to a restaurant. It's your anniversary? Go out to a restaurant. It's Valentine's Day? It's the summer solstice? It's Friday night? Go out to a restaurant.

When you get a babysitter for the children so you can spend some time together, chances are you're going out to a restaurant.

We all love restaurants. We love the elegance, the pampering, the romantic atmosphere. We love being able to eat sumptuously without having to prepare the meal or clean up afterward. We love the change of food—something different from our daily fare—fancier, perhaps, or from another part of the world. For many couples eating is a form of exploration.

New Horizons

I grew up eating a lot of TV dinners, fast food, and hot dogs. When my wife and I were first dating, she wanted to expand my horizons by introducing me to new foods. At first I wasn't all that enthusiastic, but with some coaxing, I was willing to try. We started with Greek food, and I fell in love with moussaka. Next, Indonesian — satay dinners with dozens of little side dishes. Eventually, she moved me on to Moroccan, French, Thai.

We began the eating adventure nine years ago. But today, when it comes to making suggestions, I'm an equal partner. In fact, guess who taught "Ms. Cuisine" how to use chopsticks?

Alfresco dining has a special romance about it (so much so that some restaurants actually offer outdoor dining with heat lamps!). Outdoor cafés have an informal charm to them. But there is something especially appealing about an elegant, formal table — moved outdoors.

Out Back

My husband and I have an agreement: we keep birthdays simple. No extravagant gifts, just something thoughtful. And we always go out for dinner. I like to surprise him by taking him to unusual restaurants for his birthday.

One year, a month before his birthday, we were having dinner at an old Victorian house that had just been refurbished and converted to a restaurant. Perfect!

During our meal, I needed to use the restroom and the waiter directed me, "Down the hall, down the stairs, and to your right." At the bottom of the stairs, along with the restroom, I saw an open door leading to a brick patio. One wall was overgrown with grapevines. Except for some unsightly old chairs stacked in the corner, it was charming. I wondered why they didn't use it for outdoor dining and asked the maitre d'. "Oh, someday, when we get the chance to fix it up," he answered.

Several days later I called the restaurant. Begging and cajoling, I succeeded in having them make special arrangements.

She told me we'd be dining somewhere completely different for my birthday. Then we went to a restaurant we'd been to only recently. When I pointed this out, she just smiled impishly and said, "Wait and see."

The maitre d' showed us down the stairs. I asked, "Are we going to eat in the bathroom?" And then he opened the door to a lovely private patio. The table was set with white linen, beautiful silver and china, flowers, and candles. It was a warm, balmy evening, perfect for dining outside. And we were the only ones in our little "room" out back!

ROOM SERVICE

People are virtually unanimous that hotel room service is a luxury: a leisurely breakfast brought to your room; the pleasure of a private dinner when you're feeling too tired — or too romantic — to go out; the delight of a snack brought to you, with ceremony, at odd hours . . .

Fast Food

Our flight had been held up by bad weather; it had been hours since we'd eaten; and as far as we were concerned, it was dinnertime. Our stomachs didn't care that by the time we checked into the hotel, it was 3 A.M. The first thing we tried to do? Order room service. But there was one problem: this hotel didn't have twenty-four-hour room service, and the kitchen was closed.

I had started to unpack when my husband announced, "Where there's a will, there's a way. It's a matter of price." I didn't have much hope that he'd manage something.

I could hear him talking on the phone, but I didn't pay any attention to what he was saying. For me, it was off to a hot bath.

As I got out of the tub and was putting on a robe, I heard someone knocking at our door and calling out, "Room Service!"

After I heard the waiter leave, I ventured out to see what miracle had been wrought. The room service cart was opened up as a table, covered with white linen. On it were elegant covered silver serving trays. With a flourish, my husband took the top off and there was . . . a fast-food cheeseburger.

"I knew there had to be one of these places nearby," he explained. "It was just a matter of persuading someone to go out for it." Of course, no self-respecting hotel would deliver it without the proper pomp and circumstance!

It Takes Two to Tango

———◆———

There's a high statistical probability that one of you says toMAYto, and the other, toMAHto. Because a couple is made up of two unique and complex individuals, not two clones joined at the hip, you will always have areas where you see things differently.

Each of you brings well-defined interests, talents, and attitudes to your relationship — these differences can be part of the joy of being a couple. It's exciting to learn about each other, it's fun to explore new things together, and gratifying to share experiences, as long as *both* of you want to!

This raises the question: How do you get your partner to join in something new to him or her? We posed this question to the couples who contributed to this book, and found many have worked out

"What counts in making a happy [relationship] is not so much how compatible you are, but how you deal with incompatibility."

Daniel Goleman

GETTING
YOUR
PARTNER
INTERESTED

*Plan it . . .
do all the legwork,
think of
special touches*

•

*Introduce a new
experience in
"small doses" . . .
listen to opera
selections
at home . . .
a weekend away
for the first
camping trip . . .*

wonderful ways to invite and motivate each other . . . and to participate with a generous spirit of enthusiasm. They also talked about circumstances and times when it's appropriate, *instead*, to appreciate, support, and celebrate their differences.

GETTING YOUR PARTNER INTERESTED

Sometimes getting your partner to come along is less a matter of resistance, and more of overcoming inertia! As one man said, "I'll try just about anything, but please don't make me plan it!" Quite a few couples tell stories of one partner determined enough to make it happen, and exerting the effort to arrange everything.

Planning something for an unmotivated partner takes some thoughtfulness and care. One woman told us about how she succeeded in getting her husband to go camping.

Camping in Comfort

I grew up camping . . . he'd never been. So I knew I had my work cut out for me. It took a lot of scheming, but I finally persuaded him to try it.

First of all, I brought up the idea when he was in such a good mood that I thought he'd agree to anything! Second, I presented it in the most appealing way — I suggested we include biking (which he loves) along some wonderful scenic roads in the area. Then, I planned everything . . . the meals, the gear . . . and I borrowed my step-dad's van so we'd have room to pack two comfortable lounge chairs, along with inner tubes for floating down the river.

I like hot showers and warm, dry beds. Giving them up to sleep in the woods seems like the depth of deprivation. And who knows what four-legged things might be out there with you?

But when she suggested it this time, she made it sound easy and fun, and I thought, "Aw, why not. She's done it before and she's survived."

As it turned out, I had a far better time than I had imagined I would. She showed me how to make a solar hot shower, cook delicious food over a campfire, and she convinced me that nothing was lurking in the woods. Of course, next time I'll have to pull my own weight, but that just might be fun.

GETTING
YOUR
PARTNER
INTERESTED

Make it a surprise

•

Honey-coat your plan

•

*Make dream lists,
compare them . . .
match some,
negotiate others*

•

*Make dream cards . . .
random draws . . .
plan some,
negotiate others*

•

*Don't forget to
simply ask!*

Another couple wrote they'd been talking for years about a vacation trip to the Southwest.

⁕

Santa Fe Bound

Traveling was something we loved to talk about: "Hey, wouldn't it be great to drive through New Mexico and Arizona?" She'd agree, but then another year would go by and we still hadn't gone. I finally realized that I was the one who really wanted to take the trip. So I sat down one day and started to plan it. I didn't "unveil" the trip to her until I had the whole thing organized. With the entire plan laid out before her, she had to agree . . . and she did.

◄►

I finally had to admit that although we kept talking about a trip across the desert, I really wasn't enthusiastic about the hot, dry environment. But, when he made all the arrangements, and all I had to do was pack my bags and get in the car, I agreed to go. The change from the lush green landscape where we live to the sharp peaks and ocher buttes was dramatic. The cactus and sagebrush looked like something from a Western movie set. I even agreed, believe it or not, to a mule ride down a steep narrow trail to the bottom of the Grand Canyon. I'm not ready to move there, but I did enjoy seeing a place so different from what I had known.

A surprise can be just the charm that opens your partner to a new activity . . .

❧

Throw Another Pizza on the Grill

I signed us both up for a pizza cooking class, without telling him in advance. I knew he'd never go unless I did it this way. On the night of the class I "kidnapped" him . . . I told him I had a surprise destination, and that it would involve good food! When we got there, at first he was a bit taken aback, but as he got into kneading and tossing the dough, he really enjoyed it. We learned how to make a pizza in our covered barbecue. Now he considers himself an expert!

Couple after couple suggested that a way to entice your partner to expand his or her horizons is to "honey-coat" your plan.

Check the Pockets!

For the longest time I'd been wanting her to come with me to a baseball game. But I just couldn't get her interested. Finally I tried a different approach. I bought her an attractive windbreaker, warm enough for a night game! Then I put a pair of tickets to an upcoming game in the pocket. Well, what could she say?

Not only was she a good sport, and had a pretty good time, but I actually heard her cheer at one point.

About two weeks later, she gave me an attractively wrapped gift box. Inside — a pair of small binoculars (perfect for a baseball game or . . .) *and* two tickets to see *La Bohème*.

Some couples have found more structured ways to get their partner involved.

How often we find ourselves thinking about the things we'd like to do and places we'd like to go. And all of us have probably daydreamed about something we wish we could get our partner to join in . . . something in which he or she simply shows no interest. How to use these daydreams?

Matching Dreams

Twice a year, always on a Sunday morning, always over a special brunch, we take two long pieces of paper and start to dream. We each write down ten things we'd like to do together in the next six months.

Then we put our lists side-by-side on the table and compare them. The things we agree on are easy. For instance, last time both of us wanted to get a dog, learn Spanish, and take a trip to Mexico. These went on our "wish" list and we scheduled, worked, and saved to make them happen.

For those things that don't match, we negotiate. My partner will go to a football game with me, if I agree to see a touring Broadway play with her.

We both want to get more physical exercise — perhaps we'll start walking after work, while we negotiate over buying a stationary bicycle for the den or joining a gym. We agree the bathroom needs work — but we'll have to discuss whether it's going to be paint or wallpaper.

One thing that's absolutely certain — we'll both have dog-obedience school on our next lists!

Pick a Card, Any Card

We keep two "wish" bowls in the kitchen, one for each of us. Next to them we keep a stack of index cards. Whenever something comes to mind that would be fun to do together, it gets written down on an index card and dropped into the appropriate bowl.

We've even created a ritual for the "big drawing." At the beginning of each month, we sit down at the end of the day with a glass of wine and some cheese, and we each pick five cards at random from the other's bowl. We read them over, talk about them, and negotiate a bit . . . "I'll go to yours, if you'll go to mine." The only rule is we have to agree on two activities to be done during the next month.

When all else fails . . . just try asking your partner to go along with what you want to do! You might get a "yes."

A Poor Struggling, Fainting Seaman

Although my girlfriend had never even been in a canoe, I had this idea that going canoeing together would be truly romantic. There we'd be, out in nature together—it would be peaceful, beautiful.

Everything got off to a wonderful start, until I asked her to back paddle into an eddy. She turned around to look at it. When she saw the water rushing toward us, she gasped and grabbed the side of the canoe.

She told me later that she thought she was going to faint. Well, that moment of panic was all the canoe needed. The next thing we knew, we flipped over. Got soaked. Lost all our gear. Lost our picnic lunch. We crawled up on the bank and started to laugh. We laughed until we nearly cried.

The next weekend, when we went to church, one of the hymns was "Some poor struggling, fainting seaman / You may rescue, you may save." We looked at each other and couldn't stop giggling.

Now that you've persuaded your partner to go along with something you want to do, how do you ensure that he or she will participate cheerfully, without grumbling or criticizing? Your partner's attitude about trying something new will affect how much you both enjoy it.

Smokey the Bear

During our first years together we always did our vacations my way . . . comfortable hotel, sightseeing, dinner out, some shopping, cafés, nightlife . . . very civilized.

Then my husband talked me into spending one of our two weeks of vacation in a rustic cabin out in the tules—I agreed in a moment of weakness. Then he offered me the following: we'd take our own, comfortable pillows, an espresso maker, the Sunday newspaper, and the promise that he'd do the cooking, if I'd agree to go with a smile, not a frown.

Even though I was not looking forward to a week with Smokey the Bear, I promised to try to be cheerful.

I never thought I'd say this, but I actually liked it. Our cabin wasn't exactly a five-star hotel, but it was cozy and intimate.

We took long walks in the forest. When it rained, we sat in front of the stone fireplace and roasted marshmallows. We made love in the afternoons. We had a hilarious time trying to cook on the tiny propane stove. We truly enjoyed each other that week that we spent alone in the woods.

I'm not sure this means that I'd agree to a trek in the Himalayas, but who knows? He's very convincing.

ONCE YOU
AGREE ON AN
ACTIVITY . . .

*Get right on it . . .
don't let the
moment pass*

•

*Agree . . . with a
positive spirit*

•

*Use the Rule of Three
. . . the "unwilling"
partner finds three
things to like!*

O
ne couple hit on an ingenious "rule" to assure
that the "reluctant" partner would have the
right attitude . . .

One, Two, Three

Ballroom dancing looked like another pipe dream.
And even if I did convince him to try it, I knew I'd
have another problem: How much fun would it be
if he had a chip on his shoulder the entire time? So
when I finally managed to "negotiate" his agreement to take a dancing class, I included what later
turned out to be a great idea: He had to find three
things about it that he liked. "I mean it," I said.
"You'll be quizzed afterwards!"

As long as I had to look for those three things,
I thought I might as well go with a positive spirit.
My three things? Some of the couples were
hilarious to watch (probably as awkward as I
was), the exercise was good, and I really enjoyed
watching how gracefully she danced.

Since then, we've used this rule several times —
once for both of us. We had to go on a trip neither
of us wanted to take, so we applied the Rule of
Three. It helped, or at least it gave us some things
to laugh about.

Oh, and our ballroom dancing? We were at a
wedding recently and other people complimented
us on our dancing.

*"Dancing is
discovery and
recreation,
especially . . .
the dance of love."*
Leopol S. Senghor

Even if you can't find three things to enjoy (and most likely you can, if you try), then possibly you could simply enjoy your partner's enjoyment . . .

The Baseball Kid

He's a baseball nut. While I'm not all that interested, I agreed to go with him to a Mets' game. He was really tickled to have me along; and I got a kick out of how much he enjoyed the game. You should have seen him. Whenever anything exciting would happen, he'd jump up and down, yell a lot, and wave his arms. He threw his hat in the air (says he'll get another). He was like a kid. It was another side to him, one I'd rarely seen.

We ate everything the vendors offered, and then went out for pizza. Would I go to another game? Sure, if only to watch my husband. I might skip the chili dogs next time.

But what can you do when, even after negotiations, finally reaching an agreement, and then careful planning, it still doesn't work out?

⚜

Sailors' Delight

My wife is from the Midwest and I grew up on the West Coast and on a sailboat. I looked forward to our living together in California after we got married. I even succeeded in talking her into taking a trip on my sailboat for our honeymoon.

We were tacking our way through the inland waterway when I announced that we were "coming about." She stood up to see what was happening just in time to catch the swinging boom with her shoulder. For the next few weeks her shoulder and arm had a lovely blue and yellow cast to them.

Yes, we're still married (happily), she's taken sailing lessons, including the terminology, and we can't find enough time to be on the boat together. We can now laugh about her "maiden cruise." Thank goodness I married someone with a sense of humor.

CELEBRATING THE DIFFERENCES

Sometimes the differences between you are there to stay, and trying to join each other is not appropriate. This may be the time to *celebrate* those differences.

The couples we heard from had wonderful stories to tell about how the differences between them add a positive dimension to their lives. There is obviously a lot of pleasure to be had in sharing the enthusiasm, the interest, and the enjoyment that one's partner receives from an activity.

Part of the support each partner offers the other is acceptance pure and simple — without any desire for either to change. These couples recognize that personal preferences in activities, hobbies, and even habits can widely diverge without threatening the relationship. They appreciate and accept these differences, and their relationship flourishes.

"If we all pulled in one direction, the world would keel over."
Yiddish proverb

Ships Passing in the Night

I'm married to a night owl. My wife starts to get active at 9 P.M. — sometimes she reads until 3 in the morning. I don't know how she does it . . . I can't stay awake after 11, and I'm awake promptly at 5 every morning. I couldn't sleep later if I tried. But she couldn't wake up then if her life depended on it.

You'd think this would be a problem, but it isn't. In fact, it's marvelous. We each have private time this way. I wouldn't trade my mornings alone for anything. I go for a run, shower, shave, and then wake her up in time for her to get ready for work. She loves her night times alone: reading, writing, puttering around, watching old movies on TV.

Sometimes, when I get up in the morning, I find a little surprise left out for me — muffins she made the night before or something she wrote for me. This has inspired me. Now I bring her the paper and a cup of coffee when I wake her up.

Feeling Left Out . . .

I love to spend my spare time curled up with a book or magazine . . . anything good to read. My husband is a true child of the electronic age. He loves TV— documentaries, the news, and FOOTBALL.

His enthusiasm for "Monday Night Football" became an issue. I hated it. I was feeling left out because he wanted to sit and yell at the TV instead of talking with me. Meanwhile, he felt excluded whenever I was buried in a book. Finally it dawned on us that we each needed to "allow" the other to enjoy different things. Now, on those Monday nights he has his game, I schedule something for myself—often an evening with some of my friends, a movie, a workshop . . .

We've found other ways, too, to bridge our gap. As often as I can, I sit with him and we watch the late evening news together. And I've gotten him in the habit of reading the paper, at least for a leisurely Sunday morning.

"It is a good thing to demand liberty for ourselves and for those who agree with us, but it is a better thing and a rarer thing to give liberty to others who do not agree with us."
Franklin D. Roosevelt

Side by Side

My wife and I have very different interests, but we get a lot of satisfaction spending time together even when we're not doing the same thing. We do a lot of things side by side. She gardens; I tinker with my car. She does needlework; I'm a ham operator. Even when we're not in the same room, we enjoy the companionship of just being in the same house. We touch base now and then — look over the other's shoulder, bring each other a snack, offer a word of praise when something is going well, or consolation when it's not. "Togetherness" isn't always doing the same things. Sometimes it's just being near each other.

Couples often talked about how pervasive an influence music is in their lives — people tend to have strong feelings about their preferences. And with so much variety available, it's sometimes hard to find two people who appreciate exactly the same music. Sometimes your partner can learn to enjoy the music you love. If not, there are creative ways to allow each of you to enjoy your "own" music.

The Hillbilly and the Longhair

I grew up listening to my dad strum a guitar on our front porch. We kids knew all the words to his old songs and sang right along. That music is as important as breathing to me. But my wife's family never listened to country music. She likes classical. I guess you'd say ours is a marriage of the hillbilly and the longhair!

I've tried, but I just can't seem to develop a taste for her music, and I know she's not wild about mine. Around the house we both make a lot of use of headphones. What a great invention! And when we have friends over, we put on the kind of music they like. The only time we have a real problem is when we go on driving trips.

Over the years we've had to work out a sort of pact: equal time. When we're driving, she gets an hour of her cassettes. Then I get an hour of mine. I like to kid her about her choices. She kids me about mine. But we both figure we can live with the other's music for an hour at a time!

Then, there are the *major* differences. These may require a little more effort, but the rewards are great. We heard from many couples who have successfully learned to appreciate and live with each other's cultural and religious differences. They choose to support each other's traditions, not to try to change them. And mutual support lets them see things through a new pair of eyes, bringing a fresh perspective to their own lives. As one person said, "Marrying into another culture has helped me understand my own culture better. And by being respectful and tolerant of those we love, and by bringing up our children to appreciate these differences, we are doing our small part to try to make the world a more tolerant place."

Stocking Surprises

Even though celebrating Christmas is not part of my heritage, I enjoy the wonderful aroma of Christmas cookies and pine needles, and the lovely decorations on the tree. I also enjoy my girlfriend's enthusiasm as she prepares for the holidays. I've even found a delightful way to participate — on Christmas Eve, when she goes to church, I fill the stockings with surprises.

It can be hard to have your deeply held traditions or beliefs held up to the light of comparison. We can feel challenged, even when no challenge is intended. To overcome this, couples told us how they deliberately cultivate attitudes that make each partner feel accepted and supported. They consciously look for what is positive, interesting, perhaps stimulating, about their differences. They concentrate on being constructive.

A Long, Continuous Tradition

My parents came to this country from Bulgaria, and even though I don't share my husband's tradition of celebrating Passover, I deeply respect its relevance as a reminder of the importance of guarding personal freedom. When I'm with him as he participates in his observances, I can also appreciate the very gratifying feeling of his being part of a long, continuous tradition.

There can be enormous cultural differences between people from different parts of the world.
These differences can be as simple as culinary styles,
or as deep and emotional as different family expec-
tations and attitudes about child rearing, education,
and hospitality. Often one or both families, anxious
about the influence of the other's culture, become
fearful of seeing theirs diluted or lost.

But many couples told us of their success, not only
in overcoming cultural differences, but in celebrating
them. They all have one thing in common: They
make a point of respecting each other's cultures, re-
garding them as rich new worlds to explore. And
many of them recall making a point, early on, of
reaching out to their partner's family in an effort to
relieve them of their concern. They all report that the
effort has given them rich satisfaction, a more colorful life, and a much closer relationship.

High Hopes

My husband comes from a large, extended
Armenian family. Most of them live close by,
so there are a lot of lively get-togethers and
big family dinners. I enjoy the conviviality,
and I love the food. My mother-in-law says
I'm her "best customer."

Although Armenian was my husband's first
language, he is equally fluent in English. In fact,
the entire family speaks excellent English, but

they speak Armenian among themselves. I am the only non-Armenian to marry into the family. When I'm present, they all do the polite thing— they switch to English.

Or they did until recently. I didn't feel completely comfortable with the language gap. Why should they switch? Some day, I promised myself, I'd learn Armenian. I got the impetus I needed when our daughter was born. I wanted to be able to help her maintain her link to that part of her cultural heritage, and the language is its cornerstone.

I ordered audio tapes and started going to a weekly Armenian language class at the church. Now, although I am far from fluent, I can form a sentence or two, and can follow the family chitchat. I can even make bilingual puns on occasion. I like to say I have "high hopes" for learning Armenian (there's a play on words there if you know the language).

My husband was very moved by my effort, and the family is much more relaxed about speaking Armenian in front of me now. And because they don't switch to English as often, my daughter is exposed to far more of the language. A side benefit is the fun my husband and I now get from having a "secret" language for communicating with each other in public!

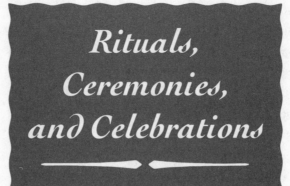

Rituals, Ceremonies, and Celebrations

For years we've made a special ritual of watching the new moon rise. Through the top branches of the trees, we can just see it . . . a thin, delicate, silver crescent gleaming in the velvet dark sky. As soon as we see it, we kiss. We call this our "good luck moon."

"Custom — the great guide to human life."
David Hume

"Ceremony — the wine of human existence."
Morris R. Cohen

The new moon, a kiss — a simple ritual that celebrates so many things; time together made special by nature's breathtaking beauty.

By observing everyday rituals, couples define their relationship. These rituals make them feel special. Their lives together are invested with more meaning. Their rituals help them pay attention to *how* they live their lives. And they symbolize the continuity of the relationship.

116

EVERYDAY RITUALS & CEREMONIES

Coffee, tea, newspaper in the morning . . . delivered by one to the other in bed . . . shared in bed

•

Breakfast . . . together

•

Daily walks . . . with the dog, for exercise, after dinner

Tea for Two

We started years ago, when we had precious little time together . . . just a bit of overlap after I got home from my job, and before he left for his. My family, being English, had tea every afternoon; we adopted this tradition for ourselves as a way to quietly share our between-shift time.

Although our schedules are now more in sync, we still continue the ritual whenever we can because it's been so satisfying. These days we usually have tea at the end of the workday, just a time of transition and relaxation before we start to prepare dinner.

Week's End Reward

Friday nights are ours alone. The work week is behind us, and the weekend activities are ahead. Our friends and family know we turn off our phone.

We enjoy preparing dinner together and giving ourselves time to slow down, take a breath, and catch up with each other.

By being conscious of our rituals, we may also recognize the need to change some of them.

The Morning Scramble

Our mornings were horribly hectic. We were getting up twenty minutes late, rushing through breakfast, or worse, skipping it altogether. We'd be frantic as we dressed . . . something always needed ironing or was missing a button. Finally, on the way out the door, we'd have to go through the daily search for the keys.

We eventually came to our senses and realized that this chaos was too stressful a way to start the day. We re-examined our morning routine and set about to change things. We began by laying out our clothes for the next day the night before. We nailed some small hooks on the kitchen cabinets to hang our keys on. We set our alarm a little earlier. Now, with more time, our new morning ritual is a simple quiet breakfast together, with time to relax and read the paper. What a difference in how we feel and how we relate!

EVERYDAY
RITUALS &
CEREMONIES

*Grace notes . . .
daily . . . weekly . . .
a note left in the other's
bag, briefcase*

•

*Phoning . . .
every day, from work,
from wherever
you happen to be*

•

*Kissing . . . always
when parting . . .
always when greeting*

•

*Saying "I love you"
. . . always before
hanging up*

*"All happiness
depends on a
leisurely
breakfast."*
John Gunther

Sometimes we elevate how we attend to rituals by making them into a celebration.

Celebrate! Even the word has a festive magic. From the first date to the first dance, from the marriage proposal to the honeymoon, each couple has their own romantic calendar of special dates. By lifting the day out of the ordinary and infusing it with energy and zest, the commemorations become markers in our lives.

Not Just Another Meeting

We first met at a business meeting and started dating a few weeks later. It wasn't long before I knew this was turning into a very special relationship. I looked back in my agenda book and found the date of that first meeting. For our "one month" dating anniversary, I made a color photocopy of my agenda page (with the meeting circled in red), framed it, and gave it to him. He still keeps it on his desk.

ON BENDED KNEE

Couple after couple said the same thing about a marriage proposal—it's an extremely important marker in one's life. Whether it's declared publicly or made privately, the "official" start of the engagement period has wonderful feelings associated with it. In many cases, the "popping of the question" has been carefully planned, prepared, and rehearsed to assure that it's a memorable moment (and gets a positive response).

The Old-Fashioned Way

She comes from a large, close, old-fashioned family, so when I wanted to propose to her, I did something no one else my age would ever think of—I approached her father and asked for her hand in marriage. She was enchanted, and he was as pleased as he was surprised!

Discombobulated

He proposed to me after we had gone out dancing. All through the evening I couldn't help noticing that although he was very attentive, he seemed to have something on his mind. When we left the nightclub, followed by an annoyed waitress, I realized how distracted he was—he had forgotten to pay! Later he told me he'd been thinking about and rehearsing the proposal all evening!

PROPOSALS

Presented . . .
on bended knee . . .
at a candlelit table . . .
with an embrace

•

Led off . . . with a
gift-wrapped bridal
magazine . . . with the
ring tied by a ribbon
to a poem

•

Served with surprise
. . . with the ring
planted in dessert . . .
with a plane-pulled
banner that pops the
question . . . with
a friend to videotape
the event

PROPOSALS

*Timed to be . . .
at midnight on
New Year's Eve . . .
after a romantic
dinner . . . at a
Valentine's Day party
. . . at a family party
. . . when certain
planets are aligned*

•

*With a ring . . .
great-grandmother's
. . . picked out just for
you . . . each other
. . . or picked out
later together*

Too Flustered for Words

She invited me to dinner at a very romantic restaurant overlooking the ocean. The occasion was our two-year dating anniversary, and I thought it was sweet of her to do this. But when she reached her hand across the table to mine and asked, "Will you marry me?" I was speechless. I tried to collect myself and finally got out a weak "Yes," followed by, "Of course, YES . . . absolutely YES!"

Home Game

We are both Michigan State alums, and attend every home game with the same group of friends. Paul had it all arranged. During the game, an airplane with a banner flew overhead. We were all straining to read it when suddenly I gasped. It said, "Connie will you marry me? Paul." I turned to Paul, who was down on one knee, there in the bleachers, to ask me personally. One of our friends then handed me a big bunch of yellow roses, while another friend videotaped the event. Oh, needless to say I said yes. I was so flabbergasted that I couldn't remember whether we won or lost the game.

Whether you follow a traditional ceremony or a personally written one, the wedding is a ceremonial statement of love and commitment to each other. Symbols and rituals of marriage may go back all the way to the roots of our cultures. Keeping these customs alive, many couples remain connected not only to their families and communities, but to a long continuum over time and distance.

Anniversaries, too, have evolved their own rituals and ceremonies. Whether it's been six months since you first met, ten years since your first date, or forty-five years since your wedding, couples told us how important it is for them to find a way to say, "You've made my life a celebration!"

Some couples observe an anniversary by repeating an element of the original event — from eating the top of the cake on their first wedding anniversary to renewing vows many years later.

Other couples celebrate by returning to where they first honeymooned, or by going on a "second honeymoon."

ENCORE!

Dine at the restaurant where you had your first date, a special date, where one of you proposed . . . at the spot where you finally both said yes

•

Wear your "first night" peignoir and silk pajamas

•

Bring out the top of your wedding cake for your first anniversary

•

Decorate the room with some of your wedding decorations

50th Anniversary Vows

My girlfriend and I were invited to her grandparents' 50th wedding anniversary party. It was a big gathering of her family, and in a very touching ceremony they renewed their vows. We felt privileged to participate in this—and inspired. We both felt it was a preview of the love and commitment we hoped to enjoy ourselves for many years to come. That night I proposed, and she accepted.

Mermaids

On our first night together as husband and wife, we stayed at an old hotel in a small coastal town. We ate a wonderful seafood dinner at a nearby restaurant and then stopped in the hotel bar for a nightcap. They served the drinks with corny little plastic mermaids perched on the glass rims. I saved those mermaids, and every year on our anniversary I pull them out and put them on our glasses. I know this is a silly touch, but it's our personal reminder of that special night.

THE PERFECT EXCUSE

Anniversaries, Valentine's Day, and birthdays provide a wonderful excuse for fantasy experiences . . . a hot-air balloon ride; a trip to a faraway paradise getaway; a fanciful indulgence. The occasion is festive, and so is your mood. So you pull out the stops a little . . . or a lot!

"Holidays are glorious times of the great too-much."
Leigh Hunt

Share the Fantasy

We could reach out and almost touch the stars twinkling in the ceiling as we sat in a seven-foot champagne glass . . . in the swirling frothy bubbles of a warm whirlpool! From up there we could look down into the rest of the room; the scene was right out of a movie set. The firelight reflected on the white satin sheets of the round, king-sized bed. Next to the table and chairs were a heart-shaped pool and a sauna for two. I felt like we had run away to a pleasure palace.

When we didn't want to leave the room, room service delivered whatever we wanted to eat. When we finally made an appearance, we took advantage of the restaurants, the romantic gardens and woods.

Though we called it our Baker's Dozen anniversary—thirteen years—everyone at the Pocono Mountain resort thought we were on our honeymoon, so that tells you what kind of week we had!

EXTRAVAGANCES/ INDULGENCES

A hot-air balloon ride followed by a champagne brunch

•

Reserve the bridal suite at the fanciest hotel in town

•

A formal, at-home catered dinner . . . in the dining room, in the garden

•

Love songs . . . sung for you by a chanteuse hired to come to your home . . . in a private room at a restaurant

*Live Maine lobster
or San Francisco
Dungeness crab . . .
airfreighted*

•

*Fill your bedroom
to overflowing with
flowers . . . buckets
and baskets*

•

*A ride for two . . .
in a carriage, a sleigh,
the bay, a gondola*

•

*Dinner à deux . . .
on a boat . . .
on a barge . . .
on a lake*

•

*Paddle under a full
moon . . . canoeing
or rowing*

•

*Tour the city . . .
on a seaplane,
in a limousine*

But the widely acknowledged occasions aren't the only times couples celebrate. Couples find all kinds of reasons to celebrate occasions of their own making.

They celebrate significant dates in their lives. These are made more meaningful when they can be celebrated together.

Many couples create their own unique rituals even for observances associated with "public" holidays. One couple buys a special type of Christmas ornament every year—"We have a collection of fourteen of these ornaments now, one for each year we've been together." Another couple, from Montana, where the end of winter is of some importance, marks the return of spring, a time of renewal and rising spirits, with their own personal gardening ritual.

Whatever the occasion, central to the celebration is the *process*—dreaming and planning it together, and making it happen.

Cabin Fever

We live in Alaska, where the winters are long and cold. After months of snow, ice, and dark afternoons, we really needed something to celebrate. Actually, what we needed was a beach — but without the time or money to go to Hawaii or Jamaica, a tropical vacation was out of the question. Or was it?

We pushed the dining room furniture over to one wall, spread two beach towels on the floor, and plugged in a sunlamp. I set out rum and cola, fruit, cheese, and crackers, and put on our reggae and steel drum tapes. We both changed into our bathing suits and snacked, talked, and danced under the sunlamp!

Two Minds, One Party

We had been dating for almost a year, and Dave and I wanted to celebrate. We had a dual reason. Susan, a mutual friend who had introduced us, had just received a wonderful job opportunity in another state. We'd give Susan a farewell party and at the same time privately celebrate our dating anniversary.

When Dave and I got together one Saturday afternoon to plan the party, I'd already thought of a few suggestions, including some recipes that would be fun to try.

We agreed on including old college friends and some work friends. We even agreed on dividing up the list to call the guests instead of sending out written invitations.

For the menu, I had envisioned an elegant sit-down dinner with fettucine Alfredo, baby zucchini and carrots, and a rich chocolate mousse. I love a pretty table; I'd get fresh flowers, use my good dishes and my new tablecloth with matching napkins.

Dave just laughed. His idea of a party was a backyard barbecue with hot dogs, beans, coleslaw, and a keg of beer.

We looked at it as an experience that would help us get to know each other better.

The party menu? We did have the hot dog barbecue. But we moved the dining room table outdoors and decorated it with beautiful flowers and our good dishes . . . Dave's beans and slaw couldn't have had a prettier setting.

We had so much fun together, setting up the party, spending time with our friends, sending Susan off in proper style, and secretly celebrating our anniversary.

SURPRISES

For some couples, celebrations are more fun when they're able to add the element of surprise. Couples wrote about taking turns being the "director" who plans and carries out the "secret" preparations, while the other delights in receiving the surprise and feels special because "all this was done for me."

A very popular "surprise" is a treasure hunt. One of you gets to plant the treasure, and then create and hide the clues. The intrigue, the fun, the lack of responsibility ("The clues made me do this!"), the small, interim rewards leading to a grand finale, are all reasons to make up a treasure hunt for your partner, or have your partner invite you to one.

Treasure hunts can be done simply or with great flourish. And they don't have to lead you far from home to be an exciting way to celebrate.

The Better to . . .

> *"Tradition is a clock that tells what time it was."*
> Elbert Hubbard

For our anniversary my wife and I usually go out somewhere special, but this time, as soon as I got home I knew we were going to have a very different celebration!

When I walked in the front door, the first thing I saw was the arrangement on the staircase: a rose and a silky robe, with a note that read, "The better to wrap you in, my dear." This was not going to be an ordinary evening at home.

Further up the steps was a romantic game, with another note that read, "The better to play with you, my dear." We weren't going to be playing for long, I surmised.

On the next step I picked up a gift-wrapped package with a note that read, "The better to see you in, my dear." Should I open it right here, or wait until I was up in our room? Who knew what she had waiting for me there! I opened it and found a pair of purple silk boxer shorts.

At the top I saw a chilled bottle of champagne in an ice bucket. The note read, "The better to toast you with, my dear."

Sexy music came from our bedroom around the corner. I collected all the items and carried them up to our room. My wife was sitting in a chair, in a lace teddy, with a big red bow wrapped around her. She was smiling and holding a note that read, "The better to love you with, my dear."

A treasure hunt can not only lead you around the house or garden, but can extend to the neighborhood or take you around town, where each stop is part of the celebration and sends you on to the next. A number of couples suggested that when planning it's always more fun to use places or businesses that both of you are familiar with. The staff will enjoy being part of the intrigue and may add some special touches you might not think of.

These Treasures Are Better than Gold

I was perplexed when the parking attendant at
my office building said, "Happy Birthday!" and
handed me a sealed envelope.

The note was from Mark: "Dear Elaine, On
your way home, please stop by the bakery at 12th
and Central, and ask for Thelma."

Thelma greeted me with a huge smile as though
she knew something I didn't, wished me a happy
birthday, and handed me a cake box wrapped in
flowing ribbons, a small fruit basket . . . and
another envelope.

I opened that envelope: "Dear Elaine, Just
down the block please stop into Wine and Spirits
and ask for Maurice." Maurice not only handed
me champagne, but a large, wrapped gift box and
my last letter.

"Dear Elaine, It should be around 5:30. I know
you're tired from all these 'errands.' Place the food
in the car, take the wrapped box, and go to
Helene's Beauty Salon. Rose will help you relax
with a facial, manicure, and pedicure. Then open
the gift box. Yes, I remembered you admiring that
dress. Put it on and I'll meet you at 7 at the White
Swan." My favorite restaurant!

Mission Possible

I got home early on Valentine's Day. I thought
I would relax a little before we went out. She
wasn't there, but a big paper heart dangled in the
doorway. The note on the valentine directed me
to the kitchen. On the table was my small tape
recorder with a note saying, "Push *play*."

"If you want to have the Valentine celebration of your life, follow these instructions very carefully. First, get the newspaper on top of the television and turn to the Personals in the Classified Section."

I did. A large red heart was drawn around an ad that read: "Bill, go up to our room and open the second dresser drawer. Remember, you mean everything to me!" I literally skipped up the steps.

In the bedroom I found an envelope marked "Passport." I opened the envelope and took out a room key from the fanciest downtown hotel. A note gave me the suite number and the time to arrive.

I broke the rules a little. On the way to the hotel, I stopped at a florist and picked up a dozen roses, but I was careful to follow the rest of the instructions. Who wouldn't! I arrived at the door to the hotel room (and carefully checked to make sure I had the right one). I slipped the key in the lock and opened the door.

I'd never seen anything like it. Hearts, candles, and confetti filled the room. Dozens of small plates of food were spread around to snack on. Music was playing softly—"Loving You" by Elvis. My wife greeted me, dressed in a fiery red lace gown. She handed me a glass of wine.

Later we shared a candlelight bubble bath and fell asleep in each other's arms in the early hours of the morning.

SEASONAL AND HOLIDAY RITUALS

Changing the calendar . . . monthly, annually

•

Ringing in the New Year with a personal gesture . . . private time together, sharing hopes and dreams . . . toasting each other

•

In the fall, winter . . . roasting chestnuts in the fireplace

•

At Halloween . . . carving the pumpkin, baking pumpkin pies

•

On Valentine's Day . . . exchanging small valentines . . . making them yourself

•

Observing the seasons . . . marking the summer and winter solstices, the spring and fall equinoxes . . . marking first fruits, first blossoms, the first warm day of spring, the first snowfall, the first falling leaves

Treasure hunts are just one kind of surprise. Couples create all kinds of imaginative celebrations orchestrated as surprises for their partner.

❦

You've Just Won . . .

"You've just won a fabulous trip for two to New York City!" At these words my jaw dropped. I'd put my exercise tape in the VCR, but instead of the usual video, a game show came blaring on. And who was on the show? My husband! He answered a series of questions and won a trip to New York for two, plus dinner at The Four Seasons, and tickets to a Broadway play. I couldn't believe it.

Suddenly, he came bounding into the room, brimming with excitement, waving tickets. "Happy Birthday!" he shouted, grinning and hugging me.

While I thought he'd gone to work, he was in the hall waiting for me to see the tape! This was his gift for my birthday. He'd made the tape himself—with the help of some friends who worked in a TV studio—and had slipped it into the exercise tape jacket. It's possible that he'll do something even more amazing for my next birthday, but it's hard to imagine what.

Kid Stuff

There is a little boy inside my husband. Hard as it may be to believe, that little boy never had a real birthday party. So I planned a surprise thirtieth birthday party for him that would be the kid party he never had. But it would be for just the two of us.

I bought all the essentials for a child's birthday party: paper tablecloth, napkins, and cups, all with colorful clowns on them; a clown banner; balloons and noisemakers. I made "goodie bags" with party favors like bubble gum, windup toys, and Silly Putty.™ There were hot dogs and ice cream, and a cake decorated with clowns.

He was thrilled — there we were, the two of us on our hands and knees in the kitchen playing with the windup toys on the floor!

One of the most elaborate and moving kinds of celebrations is a version of "This Is Your Life." Pictures and memorabilia are gathered, and old friends and associates contribute their memories, written or on tape. The result can be a moving tribute to the person whose life history is told, and a powerful experience for the person who cared deeply enough to organize it.

THIS IS YOUR LIFE . . .

Make an album, or put all the photos on video . . .

•

Present this at a party . . . invite all the participants . . . videotape the party

THIS IS YOUR LIFE . . .

Gather photos . . . from your albums, from old family albums, from the snapshot collections of friends and family . . . baby pictures, wedding pictures, goofing-around pictures

•

Gather memorabilia . . . photocopy the birth certificate, grade school report cards, childhood drawings . . .

•

Record the memories . . . go to family, old childhood friends, college pals, working associates . . . ask them for funniest memory, earliest memory, fondest memory, great quotes, favorite pastimes together, how they met . . . record it on a cassette tape to "capture" their voices

Remember When . . .

She would turn forty in three months, and I wanted to do something really spectacular to celebrate. I started thinking about making a video for her using old home movies and photos. It would also include the voices of her family and friends reminiscing about her.

I had a wealth of material. Family movies that included her parents, brothers, and other family members, some now long-gone. There was backyard footage of her squirting everyone in sight with a water hose, and a more recent vacation movie with lots of general clowning around. I culled through photo albums and came up with scores of pictures.

Our friends and relatives were delighted to help with the project. Part of the fun was treating it as "Top Secret." We enjoyed talking about "old times" (not really so old) and taping each person's message.

I had someone professionally edit and put it all together for me. When I presented it to her at a party with our family and friends, her eyes filled with tears when she told us how much this meant to her. To see her so pleased and moved was really a thrill for me, too.

Memory Book

For our anniversary I went through boxes of our photographs and mementos, and secretly made a scrapbook—a memory book—of our life together. There was a cocktail napkin that she'd saved from our first date, pictures of us before we were married, our wedding invitation, a program from a show we saw on our honeymoon, photos of us over the years — at home, with the family, on vacation, on our "second honeymoon." It was very moving to see it all assembled there, between leather covers. Working on it was a true labor of love. And sitting down together, reliving the many experiences captured in the book, helped us appreciate the richness of our relationship.

"Love is what you've been through with somebody."
James Thurber

*Photos . . .
beautifully framed . . .
blown up to
poster size . . .
put on a T-shirt . . .
mounted on foamcore
and cut out*

•

*Personal art . . .
a poem . . .
a sketch . . .*

•

*Mementos . . .
ticket stubs and
a program . . .
a pressed flower*

•

*Edibles . . . a box of
homemade cookies*

•

*Toys . . .
humorous windups*

*"When I give,
I give myself."*
Walt Whitman

Most couples agreed that finding or creating that special gift or card is always a challenge. We can't always give a "This Is Your Life" gift, but we still want to find one that is a personal statement — the most thoughtful expression of our love.

Something handmade; something you created; something you put some thought into — these are the gifts that truly show your love. A simple T-shirt with the right photo on it will be treasured because it has real meaning and romantic associations. And simply going to the trouble to give a gift an imaginative presentation elevates it — makes it personal.

And a Partridge in a Pear Tree

He was turning thirty. What would make that birthday memorable? I gave him thirty gifts, each individually wrapped, that represented the things he loves: a paperback by his favorite author, a mug with a funny picture of us printed on it, his favorite chocolate cookies, seasoned popcorn, a box of Cracker Jacks,™ a can of smoked oysters, and Louisiana cajun sauce. Then I got some cute things like Day-Glo™ socks and matching sunglasses, a horoscope booklet, a miniature fishing pole, a sun hat — he and they added up to thirty.

Finally, what do you do when you *can't* be together for an important day? Celebrate in advance, or give each other a "rain check." You can plan for a gift or grace note to reach your partner on that day, even though you aren't there. It can be mailed or even delivered by a friend or relative. Sometimes the effort you make when you can't be together is a loving gesture in itself.

A Celebration Redeemed

Dan would be away for two weeks at Army reserves. Our anniversary fell right in the middle of that time. Celebrating together is important to both of us, so we had to be creative.

We decided to "re-schedule" our celebration; to give us something even more to look forward to, we made an anniversary "coupon book."

Together, we wrote up two "coupons" to be used when he returned: one for a special dinner we'd cook, another to go out dancing. Then we each separately wrote two more, very personal coupons. We both had to admit, it was a lot more fun than redeeming coupons for breakfast cereal!

THAT SPECIAL GIFT

Multiple gifts . . . one of something for each year . . .

•

Series gifts . . . one leads to another and to another . . . sometimes leading up to you as the "ultimate" gift

•

Event gifts . . . special tickets, season tickets, a getaway

•

Transaction gifts . . . "tickets" for a massage, a car wash, a special dinner

Weekend Escapades

The weekend—the luxury of two days together, two days away from the work-week
schedule. Couples waxed rhapsodic when they
spoke about setting aside this time for themselves
since the weekend offers a truly refreshing change of
pace, whether they want to slow things down or liven
them up.

WEEKEND
HOTEL
GETAWAY
PACKAGES

*Pure romantic
indulgence . . .
a Do Not Disturb sign
and breakfast in bed*

•

*Shop till you
almost drop . . .
the evening is yours*

•

*Swing the clubs
and racquets . . .
dancing shoes at night*

•

*Mystery weekends . . .
follow the clues*

With a little bit of planning, you'll come back enthusiastic and ready to start a new week. And you'll be filled with the glow of feeling closer to each other.

A number of couples told us they actually appreciated the weekend getaway even more than longer vacations.

"She works freelance and I have my own business, so we both have a difficult time getting away from our work for long vacations. We find that a good weekend away can be just as relaxing as a vacation. We're ready to go back to work on Monday feeling renewed. In fact, sometimes the longer vacations have required so much preparation and travel time that they're exhausting by comparison!"

ROMANTIC HOTEL WEEKENDS

An easy getaway is usually one close to home. Hotels all over the country offer special weekend getaway packages, with attractive rates for rooms, breakfast in bed, and other amenities . . . flowers, champagne, robes, and room service. Pack a few essentials, board your dog, lock up your house, and you're on your way.

The hotels do it all for you. They create a romantic, pampered environment, where all you have to do is hang the "Do Not Disturb" sign on your door. You can suspend the real world while you step into another one where the focus is on nothing but the two of you (and there is a lot to be said for having someone else make the bed and do the dishes!).

A World Away

It was as if we'd stepped into a postcard from
another era. Less than an hour's drive from our
town, the inn was a world away. Wicker chairs on
a large veranda, a sundial in the English garden,
gingerbread trim and a dovecote in the back . . .
we had entered the simpler, slower world of an
Edwardian country house.

Our room, too, was a romantic step into the
past. A four-poster bed, a pair of armchairs and
footstools by the fireplace, lace curtains and a
thick hooked rug made us feel cozy and intimate.
It was just the setting we'd looked forward to.

What we had in mind was more than an
ordinary getaway. We'd brought a romantic game,
wine, some chocolates, nuts, and fruits, and a
small cassette player with our favorite music.

We ate a light dinner, then watched the sun set.
Already seduced by the environment, we returned
to our room to play the game. Even as I write this
note, I feel the glow of that beautiful weekend.

Couples suggested surprising their partner with
a weekend away. You'll enjoy the planning,
the anticipation, and the delight of a surprise; and
your partner will feel indulged and pampered. When
you do this, you're also telling him or her how much
you care.

*A weekend is . . .
"What you take
when you can no
longer take what
you've been
taking."*
Earl Wilson

145

Move Over

If I had ten dollars for each time we said, "This weekend we're getting away," I could afford our fantasy trip to Paris.

But this time, there would be no discussion of whether or not we should go . . . I had planned a surprise weekend for the two of us.

I did everything—packed our bags and put them in the car without her ever catching on. We drove to work as usual, but when she came to pick me up that evening, I said, "I feel like driving, if you don't mind." I suggested we go a more scenic way. The look on her face when we pulled up in front of the hotel where I had made reservations was worth the entire effort.

I hadn't suspected a thing! We pulled up to the hotel, and the next thing I knew he was grinning ear to ear, getting our suitcases out of the trunk. The really incredible thing is that he packed everything I needed (or maybe I only "needed" what he'd packed!). When I thought about how much care he'd taken, how carefully he'd planned, I was really moved. This is a man I'd gladly have gone anywhere with . . . but a weekend at a romantic hotel was pretty terrific.

A weekend is . . . "Recess between assignments."
Warren Goldberg

WEEKEND IMMERSIONS

*Movies . . .
make it a marathon
of the classics . . .
romance . . .
horror*

•

*Entertainment . . .
concerts, theater,
museums*

•

*Amusement parks,
theme parks, city
parks, zoos*

•

*Competitions,
tournaments . . .
bridge,
square dancing,
golf*

Weekends around physical activities offer not only a real break from the week, but also the opportunity to do something together that's fun *and* healthy (not to mention the freedom from guilt for eating all that good food!). Hiking, biking, tennis, golf, skiing—even taking lessons for a sport you've never really played before—whatever you enjoy doing together can make a romantic getaway weekend for you.

On the other hand, many couples enjoy spending the weekend together, but involving themselves in separate activities . . . as long as they're each doing what they want.

Racquets and Clubs

Maybe opposites attract, but that doesn't mean that "opposites" have to do everything together.

We simply don't enjoy doing all the same things. Our well-meaning friends comment on how different some of our interests are, but they're more concerned about it than we are. It doesn't have to be a problem, because we still love to spend time together, even if we don't do everything together.

He loves golf, everything about it. The paraphernalia, the 19th hole, the unhurried pace . . . he even claims he likes playing in the rain.

My passion is tennis. I like the exertion of playing singles, and the satisfaction of pounding the tennis ball.

So we found a place where we can go for a weekend that has good courts *and* a beautiful golf course. We both love it. We go our separate ways after breakfast, and then meet for lunch and give each other the play-by-play rundown of the morning.

Sometimes we spend the afternoons together, just noodling around; sometimes it's more golf and tennis. But we always go out for dinner together or order in room service. Two days of this and we're ready to face the world again.

I really think that the freedom we allow each other brings us even closer together.

"It's better to wear out than rust out."
Richard Chamberlain

Steamy Stories

For months we had been planning a weekend at a ski resort, and then I got pneumonia. I was recovering by the time our reservation date rolled around, but my doctor warned me not to overexert myself by skiing.

We decided to go anyway, and I made the best of the situation by telling myself I'd turn it into a working weekend. So, while he packed his skis, I packed my portable computer. And while he was putting ski tracks in the snow, I was putting words on a screen.

WEEKEND IMMERSIONS

*Classes . . .
cooking school,
where you get to
(or have to!) eat what
you create . . .
learn to sail . . .
take a martial arts
workshop . . .
take a seminar
in a subject
you both want to know
more about, or know
nothing about*

•

*Projects . . .
woodworking,
choose the wood,
make the shelves . . .
refinish the antique
furniture . . . measure,
plan and put in that
garden watering system*

∾

However, as I typed, it became harder and harder not to feel sorry for myself. I guess I never realized how dreary it would be to work while everyone else was having a terrific time outside.

I tried to stick to it, but the hours dragged by. Finally, I gave up and went for a walk up to the lodge. I sat by the fire and watched people come and go. While I watched, I imagined what their "stories" were. Racy stories, of course. Who wants to imagine people with mundane lives?

This got me started. I went back to my room and sat down at the computer . . . and began to write a story about a couple in a ski resort. The more I wrote, the steamier the story got.

Whew!

When my husband returned from the slopes, I suggested he take a hot bath, and I ordered some snacks from room service. When he came out of the bathroom, freshly scrubbed and glowing, I offered him something to drink and suggested that he sit and relax while I read to him. I told him I needed his opinion on part of the work I was doing.

I'll never forget the expression on his face as I got into my story of seduction and wanton romance — all taking place in a ski resort like the one where we were. It was worth missing the skiing.

To this day, when I tell him I have some work to do on my computer, he gives me a knowing look.

*"Nature:
The never-idle
workshop."*
Matthew Arnold

When the weather cooperates, almost everyone seems to relish a weekend spent outdoors. After work, school, or the concerns of the home, they're a refreshing change. Camping or staying in a cabin can be less expensive, and sometimes more peaceful, than more "luxurious" accommodations. A weekend of kayaking on a river, or bicycling on back roads, can be as rewarding as a two-week vacation.

And from the stories we've been told, weekends spent in the great outdoors seem to provide more humorous material than any others. So many things seem to go wrong when city folk get out into the country . . .

One couple told us about a romantic camping trip: the evening was lovely, the moon was full . . . and the tent collapsed.

Another was interrupted during an afternoon "nap" in their cabin at Yellowstone by a grizzly bear going through the garbage outside. "I ran back into our room and quickly latched the screen door. It seemed like the right thing to do at the time. In retrospect, I realize we were lucky the bear had as much respect for flimsy screen doors as I do!"

Still another couple wrote about how their friends finally revealed their special romantic camping spot, a little rigorous to get to, but worth it.

"We parked our car as close as possible and hiked up, carrying our gear, including a new double sleeping bag.

*"He who laughs,
lasts."*
Mary Poolegive

"The climb was, to put it mildly, challenging, and longer than anticipated. When we reached the site, we quickly set up camp and gathered wood for the fire while it was still light.

"We ate, cleaned up, and finally it was time for just us and outdoor romance. We lay back together, looking up at the stars, savoring the fresh forest smells, and—exhausted—quickly fell asleep."

ENRICHING RELATIONSHIPS

We were repeatedly told how marriage enrichment workshops and retreats can improve communication skills, enhance a relationship for years to come, and be a lot of fun!

The Refresher

My wife and I had never thought about a marriage enrichment weekend until, at dinner one night, some friends told us about their experience. They had just gotten back and were bubbling over with enthusiasm. We have a wonderful marriage and never thought we "needed" such a program.

A few Sundays later, I saw a notice about a marriage retreat sponsored by our church. I asked around and found that several couples we knew had already attended one. After listening to them, we signed up.

We tried to approach it with an open mind. But we each had a nagging fear that, in spite of our friends' reassurances, it would be uncomfortable.

It was wonderful; we were so relieved! We spent the weekend in a beautiful, downtown hotel (the getaway alone was worth it!). The program allowed us to spend quiet time talking . . . about our marriage, what was important to us, and what we looked forward to sharing. There was also an added bonus—we met a number of interesting couples.

Now we look on these weekends as a kind of refresher . . . something we can do from time to time.

laborate or simple, close to home or a bit far-
ther away, carefully planned or spontane-
ously enjoyed—any of these weekends away can be
a gift of time. Time that can be a refreshing tonic,
time you devote to each other, time that brings you
closer.

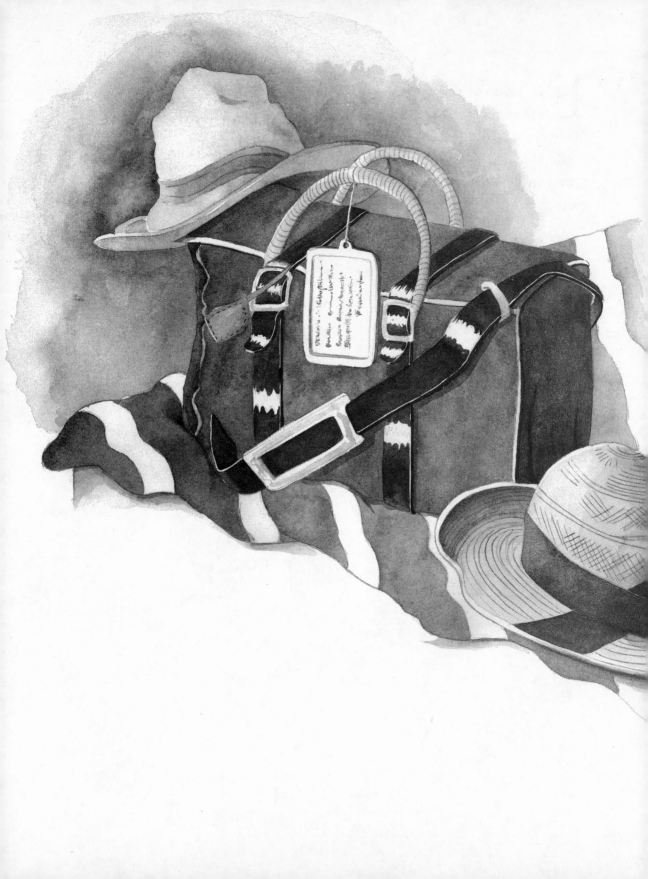

The Travel Bug Bites!

"'I've learned one thing.'
'What?'
'Never go on trips with anyone you do not love.'"

Ernest Hemingway

THE LONGER TRIP

Unlike the short getaway afternoon or weekend, the longer trip, just by virtue of the time available, offers an opportunity to do something more involved and elaborate, possibly more unusual.

It's exciting just to be free of chores and the usual

responsibilities. Add to that a change of scenery, the stimulation of learning something new, and the chance to spend days, perhaps weeks, in each other's company, sharing it all, unleashed from the constraints of daily life.

There are as many types of longer trips as there are people to take them — a languorous week of relaxation or one full of activity. A cabin on a mountain lake or a Caribbean cruise. A fishing hotel in Baja or a grand hotel in Hawaii. Camping in Yellowstone or snapping big game photos in Kenya. Taking a walking trip through southern France or a steamer through the Aleutian Islands. As one experienced traveler wrote us, "Where you go is not as important as what you put into the time together and what you both can get out of it."

By sharing extended travel, you build lasting memories that serve as "markers" — life events that function as milestones. As you travel further afield, you make discoveries, savor new sights and sounds, and sample new foods. Together, you can meet people from other places, exchange ideas, and see the world through new eyes. There's even the opportunity to see each other in a new setting — and in a fresh way.

Many couples talked about how wonderful it is to be able to reminisce about the traveling they've done together and look forward to more exciting experiences. For some, taking photos or videos brings the past into the present, for others . . .

The Journal

Some people collect stamps, others collect salt shakers. But many years ago, near the beginning of our marriage, we agreed to collect states — to visit as many (and hopefully all) as health and wealth would allow.

Over the years — and miles — we've learned a thing or two about how to make traveling more meaningful and fun.

No matter where we go or what else we take with us, we always bring a journal.

We take turns making entries. Some are very detailed, others just a note or two. But we keep it religiously. We find that writing about what we've seen and done, as well as our reactions, encourages us to be more reflective, and, in being so, to appreciate our experiences more deeply.

How many of the volumes have we read? Some, not all. We enjoy reminiscing now and then, and we take a certain comfort knowing they are there. But most satisfying of all is the actual writing of the journal entries and the sharing of them.

"I never travel without my diary. One should always have something sensational to read on the train."
Oscar Wilde

*Go back to the town
where you were born;
show off . . .
the old house,
the swimming hole,
your elementary school,
the site of your first job*

•

*Visit the country your
grandparents left
behind . . . track down
another branch
of the family*

•

*Return to the village,
town, or area where you
once served in
the Peace Corps . . .
the Armed Services*

•

*Go to the reunion . . .
high school, college,
camp . . . dig out your
yearbook and bring it
along or look through
it before you go*

•

*Make the trek to that
big family reunion . . .
or organize one*

One magical way to share the world is to literally share your worlds. A trip back to your "roots" can be a journey of self-discovery and a moving experience for both of you. A reunion, a return to the place where you spent your childhood, a trip to an ancestral home — these experiences can help you understand each other more deeply as you see them through your partner's eyes.

Going Home

Every time Norm would make plans to visit his brother in Indiana, something would happen to force us to postpone the trip. Several years had passed since he had been there, when his brother called to ask him to help get the old family home ready for sale.

Norm hadn't been home since his father died. And his mother had died when he was only sixteen. I could tell how he felt, not having his father there to talk and laugh with him, experiencing all those "going home" feelings, reliving memories, walking through his childhood home and saying goodbye to it. It was a very emotional time for him, filled with sadness.

I pretty much left him and his brother to themselves for the first few days. But one afternoon, when we had to go into town for groceries, I asked if he'd mind stopping at a craft shop I had seen the day before.

The shop had wreaths on display, and this gave me an idea. While I'm no artist, I had made them before, and I suggested to Norm that together we make wreaths for his parents and take them out to the cemetery.

I wasn't sure how he'd react, but I shouldn't have worried; he was very touched by my suggestion.

We picked out the materials together: dried roses, straw flowers, and baby's breath for his mother; grapevine, grasses, and eucalyptus for his father. The store owner let us use his back room as a workshop. When we finished, we had two beautiful wreaths—his mother's soft pastels and his father's deep green and gray.

We drove to the cemetery and placed them on his parents' graves. We stood there and looked at them for a long time, our arms around each other, without a word.

JUST RELAX

*Seek a sunny beach
. . . escape
to the cool mountains*

•

*Find a quiet town . . .
an artists' colony,
a restored historical
community*

•

*Take to the water . . .
a river, a lake,
a stream, the coast,
a beach, a pool*

•

*Take the waters . . .
a spa, hot springs,
mud baths*

•

*Take a cruise . . .
sightseeing,
educational,
special interest*

•

Take it easy

For most people, the essence of a vacation is pure relaxation, and for that it seems nothing tops a cruise. You float from one scenic destination to another, coddled by innumerable attendants ready to cater to your every whim. Swimming pools, game and exercise rooms, movies, dances, and excellent food are the daily fare. For something less expensive, and perhaps more exotic, there's a tramp steamer trip — unstructured travel from port to port on a less-than-exact timetable.

Tough Choices

We divided responsibilities with the captain and crew—they made all the decisions related to operating the ship, and we decided when to get up, what to eat, which recreational activities to enjoy.

For the more energetic or committed, there are educational cruises, working trips where you can actually assist the crew, or cruises organized around the history, archaeology, culture, even the cuisine, of a specific location.

Along with cruises, there are numerous other educational trips that are likely to provide the stimulating break you both need. From a week-long folk-dancing workshop in the mountains to a fast-paced theater tour of New York, educational vacations abound. Historical tours, restaurant tours, music festival tours, and educational programs on a variety of subjects are regularly offered by tour operators, university extensions, adult alternative schools, and professional societies. And if the exact tour you fantasize about doesn't exist, create it together.

"The important thing about your lot in life is whether you use it for building or parking."
Unknown

THE EDUCATIONAL TRIP

Take an educational cruise . . . mix learning with pleasure

•

Attend a senior study program

•

Take a theater trip . . . New York, London, summer stock, a Shakespeare festival

•

Sign up for a historical tour . . . Washington, D.C., Philadelphia, Williamsburg

"Education is learning what you didn't know you didn't know."

Daniel J. Boorstin

Educational Tour of Washington, D.C.

One part of us yearned to take an unstructured vacation. But another part was intrigued by a tour description in the World Affairs Council bulletin. Mind won out over body—we signed on for their tour of Washington, D.C.

Neither of us had been back since our high school field trips. Quite honestly, all I remember of them is singing on the bus, staying up after curfew, and the airplanes in the Smithsonian.

That was then and this was now. Talk about structure—from morning 'til night, every minute was planned . . . and every minute was fascinating. We met with our senators, listened to arguments at the Supreme Court, met with the secretary of defense, listened to experts from several think tanks, heard legislation being debated, and visited a number of foreign embassies. The entire government process became real to us in a way that no class or textbook could have made it.

It wasn't our usual kind of vacation. We didn't lie on a beach, we didn't dance until dawn, we didn't even spend time window shopping. But what an experience to share!

School Revisited

My husband and I recently discovered an education travel program for people over fifty that's gentle to our wallets and stretches our minds. Last summer we went on our first one. We stayed in a college dormitory and, for the first time, American history really came alive for us — it had been years since I'd actually read and talked about Lincoln's Gettysburg Address.

The classes were stimulating (not like the ones we slept through in school), and so was meeting new people. We've already begun gathering information about other programs. And, since the cost is so modest, even on our budget, the world is available to us. We're thinking about studying China next year.

"Don't let the golden years be the winter of your life. Let them be the harvest."
Middle East proverb

NEW VISTAS

Traveling not only presents opportunities for new experiences, but also can be the justification for trying something different. And even if it doesn't work out as planned, you may still end up with a story to share and laugh about for many years.

When Smoke Gets in Your Eyes

We took a long vacation to visit our friends in San Francisco. We really enjoyed spending time with them. But one evening, we decided to take advantage of time alone when they both had to work late.

We've lived all our lives in Miami, so for us, an evening by the fireplace is a novelty, and a romantic one at that. We looked forward to sitting together and listening to music, watching the flames and feeling the warmth from the fireplace, and, last but not least, enjoying a little romancing . . . this would be bliss.

Remembering my camping summers as a kid, I set about getting the fire started. I stacked the wood, put on a few pieces of kindling, crumpled some paper, and lit it. Within moments, the fireplace began to belch clouds of thick, gray, choking smoke. As it filled the room, the smoke alarms began shrieking. My wife and I ran frantically from window to window, opening them and trying to fan out the smoke.

We finally got the smoke out of the room, but it took the romantic atmosphere with it.

We were still laughing when our friends came home, smelled the smoke, and asked if we'd had a nice time. It seems that campfires never needed to have their flues opened!

TOO MUCH TOGETHERNESS

As a woman from California, who's logged a lot of miles traveling, said, "Okay, let's be honest, traveling together isn't always pure harmony. Sometimes around-the-clock togetherness is more pain than fun. And, if you add fatigue and sore feet, you have a less-than-perfect vacation."

A couple who recently returned from a trip to Mexico told us, "You have to make allowances when you travel. Maintain a sense of humor, and be flexible." They used "flexibility" to turn lemons into lemonade . . .

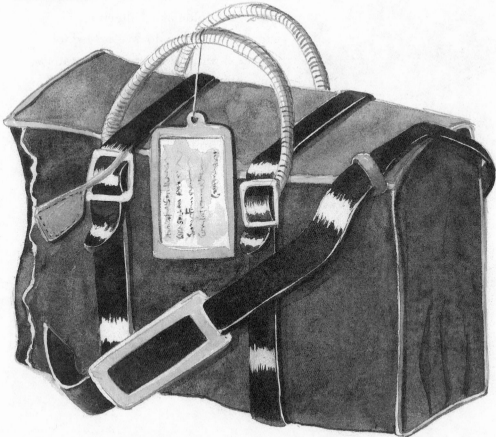

Absence Makes the Heart Grow Fonder . . .

It started when we were on a vacation in Mexico for our first anniversary. Because we're both at work all day long, we aren't used to spending twenty-four hours a day together. To complicate things, we're both accustomed to being in control of our daily activities. So you might say our "cruise ship" had two captains. Things came to a head when we couldn't agree whether to go shopping, which she wanted to do so she could practice her Spanish, or take a tour of the colonial architecture, which I wanted to do. We agreed to disagree — and to be tourists separately. That evening, we had dinner in a small restaurant recommended to her by a shop owner — in Spanish, of course. And I told her all about the fascinating buildings I'd seen. She enjoyed hearing about it over dinner far more than she ever would have enjoyed the tour itself!

Now, on those days when our interests move in different directions, so do we — a simple solution.

Spring Training

It only took one viewing of the film *The Natural* for my husband to be overwhelmed by a deep yearning to migrate to Phoenix for spring training.

Personally, I can't tell the difference between an infielder and an outsider (or is it an outfielder?), and I'm not all that interested in learning. Baseball and, as far as I knew, Phoenix, didn't have anything to interest me.

My husband saw this as a challenge. In time of need, he can be very creative, and, for him, this was a definite Time of Need. He called the Phoenix Chamber of Commerce and asked them for information about schools and courses in my two passions—cooking and gardening. There turned out to be a wonderful gourmet restaurant with cooking classes not far from the ballpark. Base hits for him, and bread and pastry for me.

We went again this year; the same arrangement. I think we both enjoyed ourselves so much because we didn't have to compromise our interests and weren't responsible for each other.

Even when his team lost, my recipes always turned out perfectly.

TRAVELING AT HOME

Even if you can't take a trip, some couples suggested you can still enjoy some of the pleasures of travel while staying at home. Pick a location (possibly a place you'd like to visit together, if you could) and read all you can about its history and current events. Sample its food; try traditional recipes. Listen to its music. Read some of its literature or poetry, see movies from or about there, even try the dances. With a little energy and imagination, couples tell us they can still share the experience and the stimulation of new places!

Grape Leaves

We have this tremendous world map on the wall in our den, and over the years we've put pins in it to mark where my sister has traveled; she works for the United Nations.

I was complaining one day that we hadn't been anywhere, when he handed me a pin, and told me to close my eyes, and stick the pin in the map. He said, "Wherever you stick it, that's where we're going."

Well, the pin ended up in the Pacific Ocean near an island I'd never even heard of. We looked at each other and agreed to try again. This time it landed on Lebanon.

Lebanon! All we knew about Lebanon was the troubles and fighting in Beirut. I said at the time, I wish it had landed on somewhere like England or France.

As if we were really going to visit, we started reading about the country. We were surprised how the image and impression of a place could change as we got to know it. There's a beautiful coastline, charming villages, and people with a reputation for being open and friendly. It's not all terrorists, like I'd imagined.

I've learned to make some Lebanese dishes. Now I'm enjoying foods whose names I recently couldn't even pronounce.

Some of the ingredients, like grape leaves, were hard to find, until my husband found a Middle Eastern grocery in the city. We've even gotten to know the owners. It feels as if we did go to Lebanon.

So Much to Do . . .
So Little Time

R omance . . . for all the wonderful things it is; for keeping the spark alive; for keeping your relationship vital and interesting. It takes time: Time together to nurture a relationship, to enhance it, and to keep it flourishing—time which is all too precious for many couples.

Lifestyle columns in newspapers and magazines are constantly telling us how pressured we are by increasing demands on our time and energy. More and more couples are in two-career households, and at the end of the day they return to their "third career": their homes, and cleaning, cooking, laundry, and often child care as well. The parent at home also experiences pressures and demands that can, at times, seem to leave little room for romance.

"Being over-scheduled is the biggest killer of romance, because when we're tired and frazzled we have nothing left for each other."
D. P., Washington

MAKE A DATE

Make a lunch date together

•

Get up a bit earlier for a breakfast date

•

Arrange a "mystery" date . . . take turns arranging and surprising each other

•

Have a shower date . . . or bubble bath

•

Make some time for "pillow talk"

"Just say STOP. It's time for us."
D. K.,
South Carolina

Can these couples find the time and the energy for romance, and still cope with commitments, stress, and even fatigue? All the couples we heard from said they can, and they do — by establishing priorities and setting goals, by making better use of the time they have, and by creating time they thought they didn't have.

MAKE A DATE

If you're dating, then you most likely already make dates; but even if you and your partner are not "dating," there's no reason to give up the excitement and fun that comes with the anticipation of looking forward to a planned evening or activity. And, by making dates, you'll set aside the special time your relationship thrives on.

For many couples, married or in committed relationships, dating takes on entirely new aspects, ones that you might relish all the more!

You can plan for a specific night each week to be your special evening. Set aside one weekend a month for your getaway. And, once scheduled, treat the commitment as if it were set in concrete.

Sometimes you need to clear the calendar — say "No" to some outside activities; stop the world and take a vacation day. Take some extra time from work — without pay if you have to.

You can make *little* "dates," as well. Meet at lunchtime for a quiet meal together. Meet after work: at a restaurant, for a walk, to "brown bag" it at a museum. Stay home, but instead of cooking dinner, order in. Turn off the TV and spend time talking or listening to relaxing music.

ESTABLISHING PRIORITIES

As one man, married for the second time, said, "In my first marriage, my wife and I put all our time into our work, children, friends, and community activities. Those were our priorities. We left no time for each other. The result? We became two strangers who happened to live in the same house. Now, I'm in my second marriage, and for these fifteen years our relationship has definitely maintained its place as the number-one priority. And because we're happier, all the other aspects of our lives have benefited."

A businesswoman from Texas told us that every time she feels overwhelmed by all those things she "should" have done, it's because she failed to set priorities. When day-to-day demands seem to be taking control of your life, you need to find a way to wrestle control back. You can begin by setting specific goals and finding time for the things that make your life richer and more enjoyable.

Wishing Can Make It So

Once a year we sit down together and make a "wish list." Over the years, these have included weekends away, getting season tickets, and taking an Italian cooking class together.

One year, as a gift to each other for our twenty-fifth wedding anniversary, one of our major goals was a bicycle trip through the Canadian Rockies. Even with our planning, the demands of work and family prevented us from going that year. In fact, we were two and a half years late.

But if we hadn't set the trip as a goal, we most likely never would have done it. And, considering how much fun — and how challenging — it was, it would have been a shame to have missed it.

"He that is everywhere is nowhere."
Thomas Fuller

FINDING THE TIME

Sometimes it's really necessary to separate the urgent from the important, and figure out how to make the urgent not quite so demanding.

Urgent . . . and Important

One day my husband, waxing philosophic, observed, "There are Important things, and there are Urgent things . . . and it's critical to know the difference."

"What is the use of running when we are not on the right road?"
Proverb

I immediately replied, "Difference? They're the same!"

"Well, that's just the thing," he answered. "They seem the same. And we often think they are. Urgent things make such a demand for our attention that we're led to believe they must be done immediately. But stacked next to the important things, they can start to lose some of their urgency."

"Like?" I asked doubtfully.

"Like going grocery shopping or going out for brunch. If we're out of coffee, bread, or milk, that could be Urgent.

"On the other hand, going out for brunch could hardly be called urgent, but it means precious time for each other. Now *that's* Important.

"Important things have a way of getting bumped by urgent things. That's why urgent things need to be re-examined. Next to something important, what seemed urgent may not be so urgent anymore. When you think about it, we can always find another time to squeeze in grocery shopping. So today . . . let's set aside the urgent and make time for the important. Where do you want to go for brunch?"

I had to admit, I certainly liked his reasoning.

And to this day, when we need to, one of us can say, "This is important." And we both know what that means.

ORGANIZE
TOGETHER

YOUR TIME
*Get a book on
time management,
organization —
AND READ IT!*

•

*Get an agenda book
. . . already have one?
Use it!*

•

*Post activity goals on
the refrigerator*

•

Plan *time together*

*"To choose time is
to save time."*
Francis Bacon

YOUR KITCHEN

Plan your meals ahead
. . . by the week

•

Do the shopping once
a week . . . based upon
your meal plan

•

Keep a meal or two
in the freezer . . .
pasta sauce, soups,
chili, lasagna

•

Does it freeze well?
Double the recipes
and freeze half
for a future meal

•

Buy prepared foods . . .
find good
take-out places

•

Collect recipes that can
be assembled with
a minimum of
preparation . . . and
serious cooks, it's not
the end of the world if,
in the privacy of your
own home, you serve
your family a packaged
"convenience" meal
now and then . . .

As another example, one couple told us that as much as they like to garden, they were beginning to feel like slaves to their yard. "Half our time was spent just on watering alone. It became clear to us that we needed to find alternatives. We figured out that we could install a sprinkler system, hire a gardener, pay a neighbor's kid to do the watering, put in desert landscaping, or replace the garden with a patio. What we finally did was put in a patio and an automatic watering system for what was left of the garden."

As a friend of ours observed, "If your days are too crowded, you can either command the sun to stand still or you can make better use of your time."

There are so many ways to use time wisely. And, as every couple advised: Organize your life. You're already organized? *Re*-organize your life. Treat your personal life like you do your business life. Use your agenda book to schedule necessary household activities, just like you do your business meetings.

Schedule in all those nagging things that have to be done, planning so that they can be done in the most efficient way. If they are still not getting done, take a tip from this couple: "We have what we call the 'Must Do Rule.' This means that after you've said, 'I have to . . .' twice, the third time you *must* do it, or forget about it. This way you'll either get it done or stop feeling guilty about not doing it!"

Some couples suggested trying to group tasks together. For example, see if it's possible to get all your errands done on one day, and plan your route so you don't waste time driving back and forth. Try to organize the major chores so they are only done on a certain day of the week.

See what can be streamlined. One couple does a lot of entertaining, and found ways to make it less time consuming — by buying a dessert instead of baking one, by preparing as much in advance as possible, and by sticking to one "foolproof" menu. "After all, it's not the same people each time! Occasionally, I change a dish here and there so that by the time someone comes over for the second 'round,' the menu's different!"

Another effective way of finding more time is for couples to take a look at how their responsibilities are divided.

The Blue Notebook Treaty

A number of years ago, my brother-in-law enrolled at a local university, and we agreed that he could stay with us. As much as we like him, and enjoy his company, it turned out to be the "last straw." The extra burden of his being in the house made me realize how resentful I was growing about the distribution of household chores.

Rather than get angry, I decided to get organized. I bought a big blue notebook and in it wrote a detailed list of ALL the things that had to be done to keep our house running smoothly: dishes, cooking, shopping, paying the bills, vacuuming, etc.

ORGANIZE
TOGETHER

YOUR CHORES
*Group your big chores
. . . all on one day
of the week*

•

*Group your errands
all for one day
when you can
do them together*

•

*Shop by mail order . . .
save driving, parking,
and your time . . .
this more than offsets
shipping costs*

•

*Get outside help . . .
a cleaning service,
someone for yard work,
a neighborhood kid
to walk the dog*

•

*Take the ironing,
and the mending . . .
to the cleaners*

•

*Examine your task
assignments . . . is
there a more efficient
(equitable) way to
distribute them?*

ORGANIZE
TOGETHER

YOUR CLOSET
*Clear it . . .
of high-maintenance
clothing*

•

*Clear it . . .
of ANYTHING
you don't wear . . .
fewer clothes
mean less crowding;
and fewer wrinkles
mean less ironing*

Then I called for a meeting of the group — sort of a treaty gathering for all three of us. I opened the blue notebook and suggested that we each review the list and pick those things to do which we disliked least. These tasks then became ours — not merely ones we "helped" with. I think my husband and his brother were somewhat taken aback by the sheer number of things to do.

Looking at the list, all those things actually in writing, was a little overwhelming. I just didn't realize how much needed to be done to keep the house on an even keel. And, until then, I hadn't realized how much I'd been taking for granted.

Selecting chores that I would now be responsible for made me really appreciate how much my wife had been trying to cope with all these years.

Even after my brother moved out, we kept the treaty in place. The result has been that *more* work gets done in less time and we spend *more* time together doing *more* things we enjoy. And it's a lot easier to feel romantic about someone when she's not resentful (and for her to feel romantic, as well).

One way to better utilize time is to learn to say "No." Many couples complained about taking on too many things, often without even realizing it. Periodically, they need to pause and think about what one more commitment will do to their lives.

Overbooked

I've always seemed to have a problem saying "no." When our son's school asked me to chair the fund-raising committee, I said, "Sure." When our church asked me to help with the building fund, I said, "Sure." When our son's scout troop needed a volunteer father for a camping trip, guess who raised his hand? And, at the same time, I was trying to develop new clients for my payroll services business.

It finally dawned on me that I might just be overextended when my wife said she was going to give me a photo of herself so I'd remember what she looked like. She said it in jest, but . . .

It got me thinking.

I began to see that when asked to do something for an obviously "worthy cause," my first impulse was to promptly say "yes." And that was my problem

In order to get a handle on this, I developed a new "rule"—when someone asks me to do something, I tell them I'll give it some thought and get back to them. Then I ask myself: How will this affect my other responsibilities? Am I the only one who could do it? How will this fit into my schedule? Is it the best use of my time? Now, when I say, "I'm sorry, I just can't do it" (and I've learned to say this gracefully), I don't feel guilty, and I don't feel overwhelmed.

"Our costliest expenditure is time."
Theophrastus

PRECIOUS GIFTS

Run an errand

•

Fill up the gas tank

•

Wash the car

•

Mow the lawn

•

Take turns making lunch, dinner, the beds

•

Take turns taking the kids to the park

•

Organize the bills

•

Go grocery shopping

•

Take the pet in for shots

THE GIFT OF TIME

Partners give each other the gift of time. When one of them has gotten his or her life organized (or when they can say, honestly, that they're really caught up), but their partner seems harried, they offer to take on something . . . an errand, perhaps, or fill the car with gas, take in the cleaning, clear out the garage. They'll both benefit . . . one feels appreciated, the other partner relieved, and both of them will have more time to be together.

WHEN YOU CAN'T BEAT IT, JOIN IT

Finally, sometimes there's no getting around it: your schedule is full, everything on it is important, and timetables cannot be changed. Don't despair; there's still hope! Try making a date with your partner to do your chores or take on that seemingly overwhelming project together. Put your calendars side by side, look for overlapping items, and see which activities you can do with each other (you might just find something that can be eliminated). The idea is to find ways to spend time together while still meeting your obligations.

A Working Picnic

My husband was working on an important project that took up all of his weekends for over a month. After a couple of weeks of missing him while he worked at his office all Saturday and Sunday, I started showing up at lunchtime with a picnic basket full of goodies. He'd take a lunch break with me, and then, when he'd go back to his work, I'd sit quietly and read a book.

Flight Pattern

My wife is a sales representative and frequently travels out of town on business. We've found a romantic way to spend time together in spite of her schedule. When she has to take an early-morning flight, we take a room the night before at the airport hotel.

We have a relaxed evening together, enjoy breakfast the next morning, and then she gets on the plane—without a hectic scramble to the airport—and I go to my office.

So, now that you've gotten everything organized and your life is a model of efficiency, take that agenda book and schedule in time for the two of you—and do it in INK.

ORGANIZE TOGETHER

YOUR STUFF

Stop wasting precious time looking for your keys, glasses, wallet, change, commuter ticket . . . get a basket or assign a place for all of these things . . . drop them there as you walk in the door, and you'll always know where to find them!

•

Get your clothes/ breakfast together the night before . . . give yourself fifteen extra minutes to start the day together more slowly

•

Have bags always packed and ready to go . . . the baby bag, the overnight bag, the picnic basket

And Baby Makes Three . . . Four . . . or More

Couples who are also parents agree that children are a joy—they give life meaning, parents can't imagine being without them . . . and they pose a challenge to a romantic relationship.

So, does romance get postponed until the children leave home? Not if you're a romantic. And not if you believe, as so many couples told us, that parents who are loving with each other provide the best environment for their children. To keep their relationship healthy and vital, and for their children's benefit, they find ways to make romance a priority.

Couples everywhere shared suggestions and ideas about how it can be done. The myth that romance goes out the window when children arrive is simply that —a myth. Granted, it's not always easy. Couples who continue to enjoy the romance of their relationship

do so because they, as partners, pay attention, create the opportunities, and exert the effort. In order to make time for each other, both partners need to make it happen. And they all agree that the payoff is more than worth it, not only in personal satisfaction, but also in creating a home and example for their children — one filled with affection and mutual appreciation.

FEELING GOOD ABOUT YOURSELF

How? Almost everybody said one way is to begin by treating yourself well! Even the little things can give you that wonderful sense of self that feels so good.

It may sound obvious, but so many couples commented on the importance of scheduling personal time — time for a bubble bath, for a haircut, to curl up with a good book, to shop for yourself, to browse through a magazine, to play golf, to watch a ball game, to just sit quietly — time for anything that helps you restore and invigorate yourself.

Finding this time can be a challenge, but as a mother of four told us, "It's terribly important that you stop and pamper yourself. No one else can do it for you." Another said, "One of the best baby shower gifts I got was a half-day salon treatment . . . an herbal soak, a facial, massage, the works."

Parents have said it's important to find the time to do things that make you feel attractive or handsome and rejuvenated — a relaxing bath, a long workout at the gym, a manicure, a brisk run or bike ride, or simply a nap.

Bath Companion

I love baths . . . for me a long hot soak is like therapy. But after my daughter was born, finding that kind of time was often difficult. Although I had tried putting her in her car seat and setting her next to the tub, it still didn't give me the precious time to myself that I wanted.

My husband and I agreed that he'd take the baby for a while when he got home from work, and I'd take a bath before dinner. I must admit, at first I felt a little guilty. He often came home tired. But he said he enjoyed time alone with the baby. And I needed to relax at the end of the day and change gears. We both found that all three of us benefited.

Sometimes one parent can take over so that the other can have some personal time. Or hire a baby-sitter for one afternoon a week so you can take some time for yourself. Many couples arrange to have the sitter come an hour early so they can leisurely get ready to go out.

Trading Days

My wife and I love to spend time together.
When our first child came along, we enjoyed
family activities even more. But with the new
child, we seemed to have little time to ourselves,
individually. So we made an arrangement—
we alternated Saturdays taking complete
responsibility for the baby. On the Saturdays
when the baby was with her, I was free to play
golf, read a book, do errands, sit and daydream.
And on her "free" Saturdays . . . whatever
moved her.

APPRECIATION

Parents tell us repeatedly that for the one doing
daily child care, the best "gift" from their partner is appreciation and understanding for how
much each day demands — energy, patience, creativ-
ity, and often stamina, to meet a child's needs and
wants.

Under Control

When my mother was moving recently from Ohio
to Florida, I went to help her, leaving our three
kids in my husband's hands for a long weekend.

I missed them terribly while I was gone. Daily phone calls helped, but it was really wonderful to come home.

I opened the door, walked in, and was struck dumb. After only three days, the house looked like a tornado had hit it! Toys were everywhere, greasy dishes were stacked up in the sink, a pan with burnt French fries sat on the stove, and later I found a load of laundry still in the washing machine.

The little one, eighteen months old, was padding about in only a diaper, with chocolate pudding all over his face, chest, and hands. There were pudding hand prints on the woodwork. The three-year-old was riding his trike in the house, the seven-year-old had the dog in her bedroom, and clothes were scattered everywhere. My husband was on his hands and knees cleaning pudding off the kitchen floor.

I'd never seen his face light up the way it did when he saw me walk in. He got up off the floor and apologized profusely for the mess. Apparently, in spite of his daily reassurances on the phone that everything was "under control," maintaining order had eluded him. He looked so bedraggled that I had to laugh.

As I hugged him, he said that now he truly appreciated what it takes to handle the kids. He kissed me, saying, "I can't believe you do this every day!"

SHOWING AFFECTION

Parents all said that showing affection for each other not only increases the feeling of romance and maintains the bond between them; it also sets an important example for their children. Seeing how they interact as a couple, their children will grow up learning how to be loving partners themselves. And a number of parents told how important it is for them to include their children when showing love and appreciation for each other.

A Card for Mommy

She was exhausted—I could hear it in her voice. Besides her job and the family, she was responsible for organizing a business conference. Now it was only one week away. She needed a boost.

I got the children together and said, "Let's do something to make Mommy feel better." We decided to give her homemade "We Love You, Mommy" cards that we'd put out on display for her at dinnertime.

I sat the crew down at a table and spread out colored construction paper, markers, scissors, and glue, and said, "Go to it."

Of course they each created a "masterpiece."

Then we set the table with all our best silverware and plates, and the kids picked flowers from our garden and made a bouquet. The cards were arranged around the table facing the door, so she couldn't miss them when she came in. Then we prepared a gourmet's delight — hot dogs and baked beans.

❖

When I walked in and saw the table, my heart just melted with love for them . . . especially for my husband. I knew he'd made it happen, even though he said it was all from the kids. What a pick-me-up!

Thank You, Thank You

When my husband was growing up, his family had a wonderful tradition. Since his mother was the one who prepared the meals, each child was encouraged to thank her for the dinner. They could say something nice about the food, or thank her for making their favorite dish . . . anything, as long as they showed true appreciation. We've made this one of our family traditions, too. Our children have so taken it to heart that when we went out to dinner recently, they each thanked the waiter for the wonderful meal!

"Children have never been very good at listening to their elders, but they have never failed to imitate them."
James Baldwin

Children learn by example. Many couples made a point similar to this woman's, married twenty-six years: "My advice is to let your children see you being affectionate as a normal part of daily life. I think it's a wonderful gift to children."

Holding Hands

At the state fair, as I walked along holding the hands of my two grandchildren, my son and his wife strolled ahead of us. I had to smile when I saw that they were holding hands.

My wife and I were married fifty-seven years, and we always held hands when we walked together. Each of *our* parents also showed their affection for each other.

You know, I see couples all the time walking along as if they had no connection at all, and it's a shame. Holding hands is such a lovely gesture, a kind of statement of unity, and it feels so good to be touching each other, aware of each other.

Loving Lessons

Both of my parents are gone now, but when I think of them (and I do often) the images that come to mind are filled with the affection they showed one another — my father coming up behind my mother as she did the dishes, putting his arms around her and kissing her neck as she giggled because it tickled; their impromptu dancing together; their holding hands when they walked.

My wife grew up in a different kind of home. It was loving, but much less demonstrative. As a result, she's quite reserved. When she met my folks, she was taken with their warmth and obvious affection for each other. Although she didn't say so, it deeply moved her. She really wanted to be able to show her feelings more easily.

I knew that she felt awkward, at first. But whatever patience and encouragement it took on my part was more than worth the "investment." And now seeing how comfortable our children are being affectionate has been very rewarding to both of us.

PRIVATE SIGNALS

No matter how close you are with your children or how much you enjoy including them in your activities, there are times when you will want, and need, to "talk" with each other privately. Many parents have ingenious private signals that allow them to flirt or otherwise communicate romantically, and secretly, in front of their children.

We're Hoping . . .

I know how you get pregnant with a baby," my four-year-old announced to me. "How's that?" I asked cautiously, trying not to reveal my astonishment. "Oh, you hope for them," she stated matter-of-factly. It took a minute, but then it dawned on me. Whenever she had asked if we were going to have another child, I had always answered, "We're hoping, honey."

Well, we've gotten a lot of mileage out of "hoping." We use it to flirt with each other. One of us will say to the other something like, "I was *hoping* we'd get some time alone tonight."

The Blue Screw

When our first child turned one year old, he was given a toy tool set for his birthday. It had a plastic hammer, screwdriver, wrench, and pliers, and giant plastic screws. Well, I couldn't resist. He never noticed that I "stole" the blue screw.

Soon after, the blue screw began to turn up . . . on a dinner plate, under a pillow, on a shelf in the bathroom, even in the refrigerator. All we had to do was see it to know what it meant. It wasn't always a signal for intimacy. Often it just said, privately, "I'm thinking of you."

We still have the blue screw. Only recently did our now-adult children make the connection!

MAKING ROMANCE A PRIORITY

Believing that personal time and time together are vitally important to your relationship doesn't show you how to *find* the time. Parents told us "creating" time requires paying attention. And it means throwing out the Myth of Spontaneity — that only spontaneous romance is exciting and that spontaneity only occurred when you were dating. (After all, how spontaneous *were* you? Didn't you set a date and time to meet? Often after taking other obligations such as school or work into consideration? Where to go? What to wear?) Many parents recall the planning, the primping and grooming, the anticipation that was part of dating, and they keep that excitement alive by continuing to "date" each other.

A number of couples suggested actually making a date. Partners ask each other out or set aside time to be alone, even staying at home. And when they *schedule* a date, they write it down in *ink* to insure it will happen. Many couples have standing dates . . . a certain time of the day, a certain day of the week, a night out once a month, a weekend away every three or six months, an extended weekend or a week away once a year.

Saturday Bliss

Saturday morning is a perfect time for the two of us to go out. Maybe I shouldn't be telling everyone (it might spoil things if everyone starts doing it), but, on Saturday mornings, restaurants are not crowded, eating out is less expensive and sitters are more available. And you don't have to worry about the sitter being able to get the kids to sleep. We've made this our special time. We rarely miss a Saturday morning together.

A number of couples suggested that in order to "force" themselves to actually *keep* their dates, they have a sitter on retainer! If you're going to pay for a sitter anyway, you might as well go out.

On Retainer

We share a baby-sitter with a neighbor. We used to compete for her . . . whoever called first for a given night, lucked out. Then the light went on: Why compete when, with a little effort, we could all get what we wanted? Every Saturday night she's both of ours. We alternate houses . . . one week she comes to our house, along with the other couple's children, and the next to theirs, along with our children. She's on "retainer," so we pay her for sitting even if we don't use her. She likes the arrangement because she's guaranteed income, and we like it because we have a dependable person always there. That's a real incentive to take the time to go out together on a regular basis! And we don't necessarily have to go *out* on those evenings. Occasionally, when the kids are with the sitter at the other house, we spend an intimate evening at home.

BOOK A GOOD
SITTER ON
RETAINER
SO YOU CAN:

*Join a team . . .
play softball,
volleyball, basketball*

•

*Reserve your time for
. . . tennis, golf*

•

*Get season tickets . . .
football, baseball,
theater, concerts,
opera, ballet*

•

*Take a course . . .
crafts, language,
dancing*

•

*See the latest . . .
movies, museum shows,
gallery openings*

•

*Try new restaurants
. . . something
romantic, something
unusual, something
that just got good
reviews*

*In the morning . . .
get up earlier than
the children . . .
shower together . . .
set up their breakfast
so they can help
themselves*

•

*During the day . . .
enforce nap time . . .
even if they play
quietly, as long as it is
in their own room*

While it helps to make time for yourselves a priority, the flip side is to be ready to take advantage of time when it "offers" itself to you.

Everybody Loves a Party

When our daughter was old enough to start getting birthday party invitations, initially we viewed them as impositions because we had to adjust our schedules around these parties.

Then it dawned on us that they were an opportunity! We got smart and made a deal with each other . . . whenever she has a birthday party to attend, we set aside our household chores and spend that time with each other. We cherish these special times alone, and she's thrilled that we share her enthusiasm for birthday parties!

All of these parents offer simple, direct advice: *Do* make a date. *Schedule* time for yourselves. Make it a top priority.

CREATING PRIVATE TIME AND SPACE

Parents told us how effective it is when they create private time by setting up "rules" that are consistently enforced. One way is with a firm bedtime, even if the child reads or plays in bed instead of going right to sleep. The children benefit from the consistency in their schedule and the parents from the enjoyment, as well as the anticipation, of privacy. And several couples commented that when they started setting a time for bed, the usual bedtime stalling and arguments greatly decreased. "Now it is the clock, not me, saying it's time for bed. The clock can't be argued with."

Other couples have "bedroom rules." Their bedroom is for them alone, the children can come in only at certain times (for instance, on weekend mornings). Another rule may be no toys in the parents' room . . . it's not an extension of the play area. Other parents may allow toys temporarily, but they must be picked up at the end of playtime. Many children are taught to knock at their parents' closed door. (To help teach this, some parents make a point of knocking before entering their child's room, as well.)

One couple told us they get weekend morning time alone by planning ahead . . . they put out the children's breakfast cereal, transfer milk to a small pitcher (easy to pour!), and preset the TV to turn on

*In the evening . . .
linger at the table
alone . . . dine after
they've gone to bed . . .
enforce bedtimes*

•

*Get a sitter . . . even
while you're at home
. . . take a sitter with
you when you go
somewhere as a family
. . . have the sitter come
early so you can enjoy
getting ready to go out*

•

*Get outside help . . .
a teenager to
do dishes . . .
light chores . . .
someone to help
clean up, or
do the yard work*

*"There never was
a child so lovely
but his [parents]
were glad to get
him asleep."*
Ralph Waldo Emerson

Save a quiet project for the kids to do in the evening, to do when the outside parent has just come home . . . crayons, puzzles, picture books

•

Eat dinner at a later time . . . so you can have a pre-meal transition from work to family . . . give the children a snack so that they can wait for dinner . . . or feed them earlier

•

Excuse the children from the dinner table after the meal . . . and from the room . . . so you can have time together

•

Establish a Quiet Time . . . no TV, no loud music

•

Enforce bedtime . . . so the parents can have time later

to an appropriate children's program. Their two youngsters are delighted to be able to take care of themselves . . . and the parents get uninterrupted time to sleep in, read the paper, or . . .

When it comes to allowing the parents to sleep late, or have private time in the morning, another couple suggests "bribery." They make a deal with their two children . . . when the kids don't bother their parents on Sunday morning, the parents will make them pancakes for breakfast (albeit a late breakfast). Besides "rules," another way to create private time is by getting up earlier than the children.

THE END OF THE DAY

Transition time — the end of the workday and with it the "traffic jam" of needs — hunger, fatigue, the children, dinner, the house. While this time can certainly be challenging, many couples told us that it can also be an opportunity.

These couples have found ways to create "quality" time at the end of the day. "We used to be drained by the time the evening rolled around. Then we started setting aside twenty minutes each night after dinner when the kids are excused. They play in another room and are not to bother us. We linger at the table and talk . . . uninterrupted." Other parents have "quiet time" rules — the hour after dinner is a time for quiet play. Other couples delay their meal, feed the children first, and use the time as a transitional period.

Many couples told us that getting "outside" help allows them more time for themselves and is more than worth the effort (and the expense). For example, one couple hires a neighborhood teenager to come in and do evening cleanup. This frees them to put their children to bed and then spend time with each other. Others, with older children, recommend renting a good video, now and then, to keep the children entertained while the parents have a peaceful dinner or share a glass of wine in another room. One couple was "driven" to another option:

Dining Out

All we wanted was some peace and quiet together. But sometimes it didn't seem possible! Finally we thought of a way.

I rented a video for our two boys, ages nine and eleven, one of the current "hot" ones . . . perfect for keeping them settled in one place for a reasonable amount of time! After they had their dinner I sat them down with a huge bowl of popcorn in front of the TV.

Then we took some cold cuts, cheese, a loaf of bread, and cold drinks and sat in the car in front of the house where we could *see* the TV and the children through the window, but not hear them. With the radio tuned to a quiet station, we ate our dinner, talked, held hands, and finally relaxed. Pastrami never tasted so good.

The baby bag . . .
with diapers, wipes,
an extra pacifier,
a container of cereal,
a change of clothes . . .
replace supplies
when you get home

•

A day trip bag . . .
for shopping trips and
errand days . . . with
wipes, tissues, crayons
and pads of paper, a
change of socks and
underwear, a couple of
granola bars and cans
of apple juice for
emergency snacks . . .

•

A beach/pool bag . . .
ready for the sitter to
take with the kids . . .
suits and towels, water
shoes, sun hats, sun
screen, some sand toys,
tissues and snacks . . .
a couple of dollars in
quarters . . . when the
suits and towels are
laundered put them
right back in the bag
(and check the other
supplies)

Many of these parents also talked about the need to make a financial, as well as an emotional, investment in creating private time. While the demands on available money can be great, there are painless ways to set aside "romantic" funds.

A Penny Saved . . .

We started putting all our pocket change into a big jar in the bedroom. It's amazing how much accumulates. Last year we used it for an entire weekend together. We arranged for one of the aides at the kids' day care to stay with them, and checked into a hotel in the mountains for one of their "romantic weekend" packages. The first evening, at dinner, we made a special toast . . . "to the jar!"

To find more time, couples suggest, you may need to ask yourself: Can I be more organized? Can I simplify my life? Maybe you need to allow the housekeeping to be less than perfect. Perhaps you need to simplify the cooking. Perhaps the lawn doesn't need to look perfectly manicured. Whatever you can do to streamline your life will give you more time for yourself and your relationship.

CHILD CARE

Every parent told us that going out for an evening, a day, or a weekend is more enjoyable when you have confidence in your baby-sitting arrangements. You can feel free to enjoy yourself because you know your children are in competent hands.

People find good sitters through all kinds of sources. Parents suggested family members, neighbors, and day care staff as sitters or referral sources. Church and synagogue bulletin boards, community newspapers, and the pediatrician's office are other sources. Sitters can come to your house or you can drop your child at a home of a parent who takes care of children, in addition to his or her own. Of course, each candidate must be screened carefully.

Baby-sitting can be expensive, but fortunately you can find creative and less costly alternatives. A group of parents can share the cost of hiring a sitter on retainer, reserving specific days and times. Some schools, community centers, churches, and synagogues offer a "movie night" (or other activities): parents drop off their children to watch a video movie or participate in other organized activities, while other parents supervise the children. Parents then alternate chaperoning movie or activity night.

You can "trade" services for baby-sitting—providing home-cooked meals, for example, as compensation for sitting. You can make an effort to get to

SITTER TIPS

*Offer a bonus if . . .
the kids are asleep
when you get home . . .
the kitchen is clean . . .
the toys are put away*

•

*You don't have
to prepare food for
your sitter . . .
snacks are OK*

•

*Find something
the sitter can do
or give the children
that they will
look forward to
getting . . . a treat,
a favorite game*

know the parents of your children's playmates, and then take turns sitting each other's children. (Sometimes this is the best solution for a weekend away.) One couple has an interesting twist on this kind of arrangement:

Nestled in Their Beds

We have neighbors whose children play with ours. We've worked out a sitting arrangement with them that is almost too good to be true. When it's our turn to go out, we take our kids over to their house, kiss the kids good-night, and take off without a care. Then, when bedtime rolls around, *one* parent puts their kids to bed, the *other* brings our kids home to our house and puts them down in their own beds, and stays with them until we get home. Not only is it terrific for the parents, but our kids love it.

FAMILY FUN

Couples tell us that the best of all worlds is when they can enjoy each other and, at the same time, enjoy their family. They picnic in parks with good playgrounds that keep the children occupied, they vacation at resorts and camps that offer activities for kids. As one mother of three said, "When we're relaxed and enjoying ourselves, it's easier for the kids to have a good time."

The message we heard over and over from couples who have children is very clear: keep romance a priority! Though children changed their lives, they see these changes as opportunities to build an even stronger, closer relationship. They recognize the effort it takes, but they value the results — a relationship that remains fresh and exciting.

ROMANCE AND FAMILY ACTIVITIES

Hotels . . . with special activities for children

•

Resorts . . . with "kids' camps"

•

Family camps . . . through schools, through churches

•

Large parks with a variety of activities for all ages . . . playground, supervised pool, tennis courts

Fanning the Flames

PUTTING LOGS ON THE FIRE

From time to time, everyone finds him or herself slipping into a routine, a predictable pattern, a ho-hum rut. Nothing is seriously wrong, but nothing is particularly exciting either; the same wake-up time, the same chores, the same place near work for lunch — patterns we seem to follow by rote.

Most couples tell us they have periods like this in their relationship — flat periods when everything seems routine.

These flat periods don't mean you and your partner are any less in love. Instead, it may

> *"What hunger is in relation to food, zest is in relation to life."*
> Bertrand Russell

mean you're not thinking about how much you love each other, or how often you're not expressing it. It doesn't mean you're unhappy, either. Probably nothing's really wrong. But if this feeling is allowed to continue, gradually, over time, the bond between you could begin to fray.

To break out of the routine, and because it's fun to re-energize a relationship, many people whose lives together are fulfilling and exciting still make a point of "re-sparking" their romance. "Re-sparking" isn't a chore . . . it's a delight!

It doesn't require a monumental effort either. Little things can light the flame: flowers out of the blue; a balloon with a message; saying "I love you" when it's not expected; making a point to tell each other how you feel, how lucky you are to have each other; remembering to include some grace notes in your lives.

THE NUMBER ONE RE-SPARKER

Turn off the TV! Almost everyone we talked with suggested this as a starting place for breaking out of a rut. TV and other distractions fill up the space between us. Remove them and almost automatically you'll feel closer. Put on your favorite music; take a walk together; read together; make a point of spending time in quiet conversation with your partner.

When you make an effort to re-spark things, your perspective changes; you feel energized and in love.

Fanning the flames can be part of a conscious effort to refocus on all the wonderful things that you find attractive about your partner—smile, voice, sense of humor, movement. For others, it's a chance to focus on those qualities that you've watched develop over the years that set your partner apart from everyone else—patience, compassion, courage, wisdom, tenderness. For still others, it's looking at your partner as if through a stranger's eyes.

*"Television—
chewing gum
for the eyes."*
Frank Lloyd Wright

Fresh Eyes

The last stop on our round of errands was the dry cleaners. I decided that I'd wait in the car while my husband picked up his suits.

After what seemed like an awfully long time, he finally came out the front door. But then he stopped and turned back. He and the owner stood near the doorway, talking. I found myself beginning to get irritated. Then, rather than let my impatience take over, I began to play a mental game.

I imagined that I was seeing my husband for the first time. I tried to notice things that a stranger would see . . . that he needs a haircut; that there are grass stains on the sleeve of his sweatshirt.

I also noticed how he waved his free hand when he talked. His gestures were graceful—as if he were conducting an orchestra. I couldn't help but think about how expressive he is, and elegant, too.

He's in good shape. He looked very attractive, standing there with the suits slung over his shoulder. It was as though I were seeing for the first time how handsome he really is. I felt my cheeks flush.

I realized how easy it could be to get used to not really seeing someone. Then he turned toward the car and smiled at me. I smiled, too.

"The important thing is to pull yourself up by your own hair to turn yourself inside out and see the whole world with fresh eyes."
Peter Weiss

Revitalizing a relationship can be as simple as tilting your head to look at something or someone from a slightly different angle. Sometimes you just need a change or two, or a little time away from your normal routine. A number of couples suggested taking something you do all the time and doing it in a new way.

❧

The Date

We've been married for six years — and I truly love my wife more now than when we first fell in love. But I have to admit that from time to time we need to do something that's out of the ordinary. So I was really intrigued when my wife called me at work and actually asked me out on a date.

She told me that she'd "pick me up" Saturday at 8 P.M. She suggested we get ready separately, then meet in the living room.

When I asked what we were going to do, she said that the arrangements were her responsibility, but I could dress casually.

The evening stands out not because of what we did, but because of the creative way my wife broke the mold . . . it may seem like a little thing, but it was a lot of fun, and different enough to be exciting.

Secret Dates

SAME . . . BUT DIFFERENT

Celebrate . . . but for no special occasion

•

*Have dinner . . .
by the fire . . .
in a different room
. . . outside . . .
late at night*

•

*Go to sleep . . .
on a mattress
in the living room,
on the deck*

•

*Drink water . . .
from crystal glasses*

•

*Have breakfast
before work
. . . out*

•

*Take a shower
. . . together*

When we got married, we decided to surprise one another with "secret dates" every few months. Whoever makes the arrangements tells the other the date, the time, and the dress. Once, to purposely mislead me, she had me pack an overnight bag but then took me to a play, meeting friends there. I've taken her for a private golf lesson followed by a picnic by a pond. Sometimes afternoon biking or a pops concert. I even rented a tux when she said the evening was formal; I didn't know until we arrived that she had made reservations for dining and dancing at a jazz supper club. One of us gets the fun of planning, the other, the benefit of the surprise.

As a couple from Florida observed, "You can change things by changing things." A new kind of restaurant, a different form of entertainment, a matinee movie. Go for an after-dinner walk. Take a study course together. Set up a little table in front of the fireplace for an intimate dinner. Wear something you normally wouldn't. Do something completely different, even something you've never done before, something you would never have thought of doing together. Whatever you do, the change alone will be refreshing.

The Jacket

I don't remember which movie it was, but I have this indelible image in my mind of Cary Grant wearing a smoking jacket. It's always been a symbol to me of all that is attractive, elegant, sexy.

Then one day when I was shopping, I saw one. Would he ever wear it? I decided to take a chance. I had it gift wrapped, just for fun, even though there was no special occasion.

He opened it, and I could tell from the expression on his face that he didn't know what to say. He wasn't sure how to feel about it, so I just put my arms around him and said, "Please wear it just once, for me."

Well, he did. And when I told him how sexy and terrific he looked in it, he got flustered (just the way I'd hoped he would).

Sometimes the desire to make a change or add something new to your life can be the impetus for a truly dramatic gesture.

Tent Magic

I saw a trail of notes. With each note I found something: first, a bottle of wine . . . then two glasses . . . then a plate of fruits and cheeses beautifully arranged . . .

The notes directed me to the front of our bedroom door. The note on the door said to knock three times. I did and was invited in.

I couldn't believe it! My husband had completely covered the bed with a tent made out of sheets stapled to the ceiling! Under the tent, the bed was made up with satin sheets. There was a silver tray with sweets and flowers on it. Even the music was dramatic. I felt like we were floating away on a magic carpet.

Re-sparking can be simply changing your environment—putting fresh flowers on the breakfast table, turning on some romantic music, or making your bedroom a more attractive, sensuous environment for the two of you.

The Room

Our house is something less than an estate, and room for storage is always a problem. Unfortunately, we had gotten into the habit of dumping things in our bedroom. After all, who would see them there? Just us, that's all.

We had our skis leaning in one corner. In another, two boxes of clothes I'd been meaning to give away. The mending. The ironing board. A stack of department store bags that were too good to throw away. That sort of stuff.

Then one evening I heard someone on TV say that the most inviting room in your house should be the bedroom. That hit home.

It didn't take much effort to convince my husband that our lives would be far more romantic if the bedroom looked more like a boudoir than a storage shed.

I started with some inexpensive particle board cabinets to set up for storage in the garage — that's where all the clutter went.

Then I put my imagination to work. I moved a cozy armchair in from the den, had it reupholstered, and bought matching sheets and shams. The final touch was airy white curtains that are light enough to wave in the breeze. What a difference! It cost less than a vacation, and now the room is light, peaceful, and uncluttered . . . and just for us.

Couples suggested changes in personal style to re-spark a relationship . . . a new fragrance, hairstyle, a washable tattoo, something different to wear. And, like anything else you do together, even if your best laid plans go awry, you'll still have something to laugh over together!

Dressing the Part

I'd always wanted to surprise my husband at the door wearing something alluring. Then I had the perfect opportunity to do it—he was out all day helping his brother work on his boat. I had plenty of time to get ready.

Right before he was expected home, I filled the bathtub with hot water—I knew he'd love that after a day of messing around on a boat. Then I changed into my outfit: a black lace teddy, high heels, and net stockings.

I heard his truck pull up. I could hardly contain myself as I stood waiting for him holding a bunch of balloons that said "I Love You!" He seemed to take forever, but finally, I heard his footsteps on the porch. I slowly opened the door, striking a lazy, sexy pose . . .

My brother and I had been working on his boat all day. He came home with me to pick up some tools he needed. I had to get a few things out of the truck, so I told him to go on into the house. The next thing I heard was my wife shrieking, and my brother came running back to the truck, looking extremely embarrassed.

I'm sorry I missed it. From what I could gather, she went flying down the hall, balloons everywhere. My brother mumbled something about my being a lucky man.

Duffle's Surprise

I was shopping one day, taking care of all the mundane errands that seem to accumulate, when I went into a department store to get socks for him and underwear for me. I was in the lingerie department waiting for an available cashier. In front of me was a big display of garter belts and slinky loungewear.

Next thing I knew, I chose something particularly provocative, saying to myself that it was time for a change! At the salesclerk's suggestion, I also bought black satin two-inch high-heeled mules. This would be fun. That night I would leave my flannel gown and big, fuzzy slippers in the closet.

As soon as I got home, I tried on my new purchases in front of the mirror, practicing my most seductive walk. I knew my husband would love it.

RE-SPARKER RECIPES

Turn off the TV!

•

Get out of town

•

Wear something completely different

•

Don't think, just do!

•

A candlelight dinner . . . with the least amount of clothing that the temperature permits (hmmm, turn up the thermostat?)

•

Revisit an old, familiar place where you shared a lot of happy times . . . a restaurant . . . a lookout point . . . a theater . . .

"Brevity is the soul of lingerie."
Dorothy Parker

RE-SPARKER
RECIPES

*Reminisce . . .
it brings smiles
to your faces!*

•

*Listen to "oldies"
and dance together*

•

*Take the time to show
that you care . . .
an act of kindness or
consideration
will fan the fire
in a relationship*

Friday night was the night. I went upstairs to set the mood. I changed into the new outfit, turned on some sultry music, lit the candles, and turned off the lights. Then I called him.

As he walked into the room, I slinked toward him with my best "come hither" look. My new satin heels wobbled, but I don't think he noticed. He definitely looked impressed.

Elated by his admiration, I felt wonderfully, confidently sexy . . . until—I tripped over Duffle, our aging, overweight Spaniel, who was too deaf to hear me coming. I tried to catch my footing, but the fancy high-heeled slippers were useless, and I fell over a table, slightly cutting my lip.

It was a while before we could stop laughing. Then we put Duffle out and got back into "the mood." My husband still asks for a repeat performance.

ROLE-PLAYING

We automatically add energy to our relationship when we change our environment. We get re-charged by changing our everyday routine," wrote a couple who've been together for fifteen years.

By making these changes, you can get back in touch with the feelings that make your relationship exciting.

Sometimes the getaway can be one of the imagination. For example, the fun of planned role-playing such as dressing as if it were prom night or "acting out" a scene in a movie. Elaborate plans, unusual combinations, exotic places, fanciful props—these can all be electrically charged, re-energizing the moment, your feelings, and your relationship.

Hollywood Beckons

We went to a Halloween costume party dressed as Batman and Batwoman. We had so much fun "being" other characters for the evening that it gave us the idea to role-play just with each other.

Though we've enjoyed a range of roles, one of my favorites is about the actor or actress trying out for a part.

One of us is trying out, the other is the director. Here's how it works: The week before, we draw straws for parts. The director is in charge of renting a video camera for the night and selecting or writing a "script." They can be taken from a play, a book, the newspaper, or an original piece, which are sometimes the funniest.

The actor or actress reads the "script" and then must come to the tryout with an appropriate "costume" and, if necessary, props (almost always simple).

These "auditions" sometimes take all evening because of the number of "takes" that are needed.

ROLE-PLAYING

Get the props from around the house . . . wander into a costume shop . . .

•

Mardi Gras . . . Halloween . . . The Black Cat . . . The Bionic Man

•

A night in the South Seas . . . with music and coconut drinks

•

The curtain goes up . . . the spotlight is on the two of you! Try a short scene from your favorite movie or play . . .

•

Think of your partner as Michelangelo, Rodin, or Picasso . . .you are the model . . . pose for the artist

The Rendezvous
I know a dark secluded place;
A place where no one knows your face;
A glass of wine, a fast embrace . . .
Hernando's Hideaway. —Adler-Ross

One day, when I found myself humming this song, I started thinking about the lyrics and took them to heart.

I wrote my husband a note, in flaming red ink, suggesting that he meet me at a cozy little bar in the lobby of a charming old hotel in the middle of town. I noted the time we'd meet and even which booth.

I came in a few minutes "late." In the soft light, I could see him sitting in the appointed place.

"Excuse me," I asked coyly. "Are you alone?"

He looked straight at me, blinked once and, slipping into his role, said, "I was."

I asked him if he came to town often, stayed in this hotel, liked his work, traveled much, was expecting to meet someone.

I don't think I need to tell you about the rest of the evening. We talked for a while, then I enticed him up to the room I had reserved earlier. We spent a wonderful night together. In the morning I suggested we part without telling each other our names.

That night, when he came home from work, neither he nor I said a word about our rendezvous . . . we didn't need to.

Six Satin Strings to Tie Around Your Finger

In reading and organizing the wealth of information we accumulated for this book, it became clear to us that romance is a state of mind. At the same time, it seems that there's a pattern to the way couples stay romantically mindful. They use, consciously or not, six "strings" — reminders of how feeling romantic brings with it excitement, warmth, and joy. We offer these "strings" to tie around your finger.

1. BEING ATTENTIVE . . .
AWARE

*"If I were to begin
life again,
I should want
it as it was.
I would only
open my eyes
a little more."*

Jules Renard

The richness is in the details. Being aware of your world and the people in it is the difference between looking and seeing, hearing and listening. By paying attention, you allow yourself to appreciate all of the things that make your life and relationship more satisfying . . . more exciting.

"**W**e've been together over twenty years and because we pay attention to romance, we are closer and more in love each year of our shared lives. How exciting the future is."

 F. S., Phoenix, Arizona

"**M**y last marriage atrophied in seven years from lack of attention and taking each other for granted. Now, in this relationship, we both pay attention to avoid ruts."

 P. F., Greeley, Colorado

2. BEING APPRECIATIVE . . .
CONSIDERATE

By sharing your love and communicating your feelings, you enrich your relationship and yourself. A gentle touch, a letter, a flower, a thoughtful gesture or spoken word—letting your partner know how much he or she is loved and appreciated gives meaning to both your lives.

"My wife and I have been married for twenty-six years. Obviously during this time, we've had many ups and downs. We've learned that the everyday things you do for each other keep romance alive and growing."

R. S., Overland Park, Kansas

"My partner is the great love of my life. The more you show your appreciation for your mate the better the relationship becomes . . . and the more your partner gives back to you."

K. R., Farmington, Missouri

"When you feel something special about the person, *tell them now* . . . we all need to hear nice things. They're like gifts we give to one another."

S.B., Chagrin Falls, Ohio

3. BEING TOGETHER...
BUILDING A PARTNERSHIP

A partnership is grounded on common goals and mutual understanding. But reaching a meeting of the minds takes effort. Being sensitive to your partner's wants and interests tells him or her that you're committed to maintaining the connection between you — one that allows you both to communicate freely and lovingly.

"Loving is not just looking at each other, it's looking in the same direction."

Antoine de
Saint-Exupéry

"Success in marriage does not come merely through finding the right mate, but through being the right mate."

Samuel Silver

"I long ago realized that if I wanted a good wife, I had better try to be an equally good man and husband." M. B., Tacoma, Washington

4. BEING YOURSELF...
CELEBRATING TWO INDIVIDUALS

The most successful couples seem to be able to maintain a balance between their partnership and their individuality. They don't forget who they are. And they respect the differences between them. Romance, and a relationship, can flourish only when the needs of the partnership *and* the individual are met.

In *Greener Pastures*, it's described this way: "To keep the fire burning brightly, there's one easy rule: Keep the two logs together, near enough to keep each other warm and far enough apart — finger's breadth — for breathing room. Good fire. Good marriage. Same rules."

"We do not receive wisdom, we have to discover it for ourselves by a voyage that no one can take for us, a voyage that no one can spare us."
Marcel Proust

"Building the relationship is not my job or her job, but our job. I do my part and allow and encourage her to do hers, in her own way. The rest is magic."
M. M., Boston, Massachusetts

5. FINDING HUMOR...
LAUGHING TOGETHER

"Humor is the ability to see three sides of one coin."
Ned Rorem

"Anger separates people, laughing brings them together."
S. A., Coeur d'Alene, Idaho

Your life and relationship can sometimes become too intense. By stepping back for a moment, not taking yourself too seriously, and learning to look for humor in a situation, you can reduce tension, dissipate anger, and become more attractive to yourself and your partner.

Occasionally you may want to keep in mind Ogden Nash's advice:

> To keep a marriage brimming
> With love in the marriage cup,
> Whenever you're wrong, admit it;
> Whenever you're right, shut up.

Or that of Piet Hein:

> The road to wisdom?
> Well, it's plain
> and simple to express:
> Err
> and err
> and err again,
> but less
> and less
> and less.

6. BEING INTIMATE . . .
BEING AFFECTIONATE

It's the possibility of physical intimacy that gives romance its piquancy. However, being romantic doesn't require physical intimacy. But the expectancy, the potential of such intimacy can energize a relationship. Letting your partner know how desirable he or she is deepens the romantic commitment between you.

"**I** can see the difference between this marriage and my last one. This time around, we're both making an effort to keep the spark alive. Intimacy thrives, and is much more satisfying when you create a romantic environment. . . . It's better than any aphrodisiac." B. L., San Antonio, Texas

"Talk not of wasted affection, affection never was wasted."
Henry Wadsworth Longfellow

"Devils can be driven out of the heart by the touch of a hand on a hand, or mouth on a mouth."
Tennessee Williams

Authors

Barbara and Michael Jonas are the creators of the romantic game *An Enchanting Evening*.™

Married for twenty-nine years, they work together as co-principals of Games Partnership Ltd., Inc., which was chosen 1992 Game Industry Manufacturer of the Year by The Game Retailer Network. They have also developed two other award-winning games: *Getting to Know You . . . Better*™ and *You Just Became a Millionaire*.™

In addition to their business experience, they served together as Peace Corps volunteers in Ghana, West Africa, and worked in the Chuuk Islands in Micronesia and on a kibbutz in Israel.

And if they've learned anything about relationships over the years, it's that love, romance, and marriage only flourish when cared for and nurtured. A well-developed sense of humor doesn't hurt, either.

Barbara Bricklin Jonas and Michael D. Jonas

Games Couples Like to Play

AN ENCHANTING EVENING™

Dim the lights. Add soft music, candlelight, some tantalizing edibles, your favorite beverage, and *An Enchanting Evening*, the romantic board game for two. These are the ingredients for the most romantic evening you'll ever spend.

How Is An Enchanting Evening™ *Played?*

The game begins with each player writing down a "secret" wish that can be shared with his or her partner that evening. The players then move around the board—drawing the card that matches the space they land on. The game's cards direct the players' actions.

Some cards ask for verbal responses, which are positive and supportive. Other cards suggest gentle touching, some playful, others subtle and ambiguous. All cards allow the players to enjoy the game, and each other, at any level of intimacy that is comfortable and fun for both of them.

The first player to reach "Finish" gets his or her wish fulfilled. (However, all players seem to agree that both players win!)

GETTING TO KNOW YOU . . . BETTER™

The award-winning game designed for two — dating, married, or just friends — to share, discover, and learn more about one another.

How Is Getting To Know You . . . Better™ *Played?*

The game begins with each player choosing a prize from a list of fourteen activities; e.g., a concert, sporting event, home-cooked dinner, or morning walk. As players move around the board, they answer questions about their life experiences, preferences, wishes, attitudes, and humorous childhood memories. Some cards offer the players an opportunity to guess what their partner would select as his/her choice. The first person to reach the end wins the opportunity for their partner to plan the activity that they selected. Since both players participate in the activity that the winner chooses, both players actually win!

An Enchanting Evening™ and *Getting To Know You . . . Better*™
are available in game, gift, and lingerie stores, as well as in
the lingerie department of many major department stores.
For store locations, information about the games,
or to order directly, you may call us toll-free at
[800] 776-7662 or [415] 495-4411 or write to us at:

Games Partnership Ltd., Inc.
116 New Montgomery Street, Suite 500
San Francisco, CA 94105

VISA, MasterCard, checks, and money orders accepted.
Price per game is $25.00,° plus $4 for shipping and handling.

°California residents, please add 8.25% sales tax to order.

To Our Readers:
We'd very much like to hear your comments about
The Book of Love, Laughter & Romance;
and your "romantic" suggestions so that
we can offer them to other couples in future editions.